GRAPPLE jr. high

TACKLING TOUGH QUESTIONS ABOUT
GOD, OTHERS, AND ME

POWERFUL WORDS

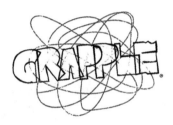

Grapple® Jr. High: Powerful Words
Copyright © 2011 Group Publishing, Inc.

group.com
simplyyouthministry.com

Unless otherwise indicated, all Scripture quotations are taken from the Holy Bible, New Living Translation, copyright © 1996, 2004, 2007. Used by permission of Tyndale House Publishers, Inc., Carol Stream, Illinois 60188. All rights reserved.

ISBN 978-0-7644-7546-7

10 9 8 7 6 5 4 3   20 19 18 17 16 15 14

Printed in the United States of America.

TABLE OF CONTENTS

INTRODUCTION

GRAPPLE® JR. HIGH

Some of your students may already seem jaded about the Bible, and some of them have never cracked one open. Wherever your teenagers are in their spiritual journey, two things they all have in common are an inquisitive mind and a need for Christ-centered biblical depth. Grapple Jr. High is specifically designed to get junior highers grappling with tough topics in meaningful ways so they understand and own their faith. Each week, students engage with memorable Bible passages and characters, grapple with the issues that come to the surface, and discover a path that leads them straight to Jesus Christ.

During class, students follow the same schedule each week.

GRAPPLE SCHEDULE

5 MINUTES	HANG TIME
10 MINUTES	GRAPPLE CHAT
10-15 MINUTES	GRAPPLE TIME
20-25 MINUTES	TEAM TIME
10 MINUTES	TEAM REPORTS
5 MINUTES	PRAYER & CHALLENGE

Please note that times are approximate and should be flexible to fit your classroom needs.

WHAT HAPPENS?
GRAPPLE HANG TIME:

Kids enjoy snacks and friendship as they spend time getting to know each other as music plays in the background. Then play a three-minute countdown, included on your Grapple DVD, to let students know how much time they have until Grapple Hang Time is over. You can also use the countdowns to wrap up an activity in the lesson.

GRAPPLE CHAT:

Chat topics connect students to one another and to the Word of God. Two topics in each lesson are built on passages or characters from the Bible, and two topics challenge students to discuss their lives. Encourage students to choose one question from each of these categories. In each lesson, Questions 1 and 3 are the biblically based questions, and Questions 2 and 4 are the ones that tap into their personal experiences.

GRAPPLE TIME:

Grapple Time is the leader-led experience for your entire class. Grapple Time involves everyone in making discoveries; the experience helps students cultivate the desire to dig into the Bible for answers.

GRAPPLE TEAM TIME:

Students get into their Grapple Teams of six or fewer to dig into the Bible with the reproducible Grapple Team Guide.

Who leads a Grapple Team? If you have six or fewer students, have them stay together with you as the leader. If you have several Grapple Teams, try these ideas: Facilitate all the teams by moving from team to team, assign a student to be the team leader, or recruit adults or high school students to be team leaders.

GRAPPLE TEAM REPORTS:

Teams vote on how they want to report what they discovered during Grapple Team Time. Once teams are ready to report, they get with other teams that chose the other style of reporting. They then take turns reporting what they learned. If you have just one Grapple Team, consider dividing your team into two smaller groups to create and present reports.

GRAPPLE PRAYER AND CHALLENGE:

Kids choose, as a class, which prayer option they would like to do. After the class closes in prayer, give kids the weekly Grapple Challenge to live out their faith during the coming week.

ALLERGY ALERT

This guide may contain activities that include food. Be aware that some kids have food allergies that can be dangerous. Know the students in your class, and consult with parents about allergies their kids may have. Also be sure to carefully read food labels, as hidden ingredients can cause allergy-related problems.

WORD!!

Who Came Up With This?
The Point: The Bible Is Inspired by God
The Passages: Matthew 5:17; John 21:24-25; 2 Timothy 3:16-17;
 2 Peter 1:2-21

GET STARTED
Lesson 1. Who Came Up With This?

GRAPPLE SCHEDULE

5 MINUTES	HANG TIME
10 MINUTES	GRAPPLE CHAT
10-15 MINUTES	GRAPPLE TIME
20-25 MINUTES	TEAM TIME
10 MINUTES	TEAM REPORTS
5 MINUTES	PRAYER & CHALLENGE

SUPPLIES
Bibles, Grapple DVD, DVD player, music CD, CD player, copy of the Grapple Team Guide for each person, paper, pens or pencils

BIBLE BASIS FOR TEACHERS
The Passage: 2 Timothy 3:16-17
From this passage it seems clear that Timothy had grown up being taught from the Scriptures, which at the time of Timothy's childhood consisted only of what we know as the Old Testament. In 2 Timothy 1:5, Paul even mentions the faith held by Timothy's mother and grandmother, which had been passed on to Timothy. From the time he was a small child, Timothy knew the Word of God.

In 2 Timothy 3, Paul goes on to emphasize the importance and reliability of God's Word. As mentioned, the Scriptures Timothy knew as a child were just the Old Testament books. However, from 2 Peter 3:15-16 we see that at about the time this letter was written, Paul's writings were being lumped together with "other parts of Scripture," indicating that they were at least beginning to be accepted by Christians as "inspired by God." Certainly Paul's statement in 2 Timothy 3:16 regarding "all Scripture" applies to the whole of what we know as the Bible today.

How does this relate to the Grapple Question? The term "inspired by God" assures us that God was involved in the writing of the Bible as he worked through human authors. That assurance helps us know that what we have in the Bible today is what God wants us to have. It tells us everything about him that he wants us to know. If we study it carefully and use it as our source for teaching, correcting, preparing, and equipping, we'll not only learn about God, but we'll also get to know God in a special and personal way. So even though kids may wonder who came up with this book and whether it's even worth perusing, they can be assured that God had a very big part in "coming up with" the Bible.

How does this connect to Jesus? Jesus is the Word made flesh (see John 1:1-4). Because Jesus is the revealed Word of God, we can be assured that all that he said and did is a glimpse into the nature of God as well as the applicability and power of Scripture. Jesus said that he did not come to abolish Scripture, but to fulfill it (see Matthew 5:17). Not only is Jesus the Living Word, Jesus also referred to Scripture frequently while he ministered on earth. If Scripture held power and authority for Jesus, it should hold that same power and authority for us today.

GRAPPLE HANG TIME: 5 MINUTES
Play music as kids enjoy snacks and friendship, and then play an opening countdown from the Grapple DVD to wrap up Grapple Hang Time.

GRAPPLE CHAT: 10 MINUTES
Have students form pairs; if you have an uneven number of kids, it's OK to have one trio in the mix. Ask each group to chat about two of the four topics below that relate to today's grapple topic. (Answers in parentheses are samples.)

IN PAIRS
Chat 1: Discover how many books are in the Old Testament and in the New Testament. (39 in the Old Testament; 27 in the New Testament)

Chat 2: How many books, of any kind, have you read since the beginning of this year?

Chat 3: Find the book of the Bible, other than Genesis, that starts with the words "In the beginning." (Gospel of John)

Chat 4: What is your favorite book of the Bible, and why?

GRAPPLE TIME: 10-15 MINUTES
Get ready: Cue the Grapple DVD to "Who Wrote It?"

Lead the entire class in the following:
Have kids form two teams.

I am going to read some famous quotes, but I'll leave out a word. Your job is to fill in the blank—or blanks.

Give students a chance to guess each missing word. Then reveal the correct word.

1. Writer Mark Twain said this: "The reports of my _____ are greatly exaggerated." (death)

2. President Abraham Lincoln said this: "My father taught me to work; he did not teach me to _____ it." (love)

3. Comedian Rodney Dangerfield said this: "I tell ya when I was a kid, all I knew was rejection. My _____, it never came back." (yo-yo)

4. Albert Einstein said this: "If the _____ don't fit the theory, change the _____." (facts)

5. Founding Father and inventor Benjamin Franklin said this: "Fish and _____ stink after three days." (visitors)

6. Actor Steve Martin said this: "You say…how can I be a millionaire…and never pay taxes? First, get a _____." (million dollars)

7. Comedian Robin Williams said this: "Ah...so many_____, so little time..." (pedestrians)

IN PAIRS
How does one word change everything? What if the Bible were a fill-in-the-blanks book? What would that be like?

TELL ALL
Share your answers.

GET READY
Distribute pens or pencils.

IN PAIRS
Fill in the blanks in these verses with your own words. Don't look up the verse in your Bible until you have guessed the missing words from all three verses. Discuss with your partner how your words would change the meaning.

Mark 10:27: "Everything is _____ with God." (possible)

Luke 9:23: "If any of you wants to be my follower, you must turn from your _____ ways, take up your _____ daily, and follow _____." (selfish; cross; me)

John 10:10: "My purpose is to give them a rich and satisfying _____." (life)

Let's watch a video that digs into who wrote the Bible.

Show the "Who Wrote It?" clip on the Grapple DVD.

The Bible was written by a bunch of farmers, old guys, and fishermen. Why should we base our lives on their opinions and musings? Why didn't God just write the Bible and send it down to us? Why did God even have to use people to help him write the Bible? Let's grapple with that.

GRAPPLE TEAM TIME: 20-25 MINUTES

Break into Grapple Teams. Encourage Grapple Team leaders to check in with kids about their week. Grapple Team leaders will facilitate discussion, using the Grapple Team Guide on pages 7-10. Afterward, students will report what they learned.

GRAPPLE TEAM REPORTS: 10 MINUTES

At the end of Grapple Team Time, match Grapple Teams that chose Option 1 with Grapple Teams that chose Option 2 from pages 9-10. Have teams present their reports. (If you have an uneven number of teams, simply form one group of three teams for the presentations. If you have only two Grapple Teams, simply do the presentations one team at a time.)

GRAPPLE PRAYER AND CHALLENGE: 5 MINUTES

Read the Grapple Prayer options. Have the class choose one prayer option that everyone will do. Allow students time to pray about what they discovered. Then close in prayer.

GET READY

For Option 2, distribute paper and make sure students have pens or pencils.

Option 1: Lectio Divina

Get comfortable, preferably sitting apart from each other. Read a Bible passage aloud, and then remain in silence for a few minutes and think about the verses. Close your eyes and breathe deeply. Then read aloud Romans 8:35-39, slowly and with feeling. Then read it two more times the same way. Finally, allow a few minutes to silently bask in God's love.

Option 2: Letter Prayers

Write a letter to Jesus. Tell him what you know is true about him and what you're unsure about; ask for his strength and help in developing a deeper trust in him.

GRAPPLE CHALLENGE

The Bible is my favorite book, but I didn't always feel that way. It took me a while to truly appreciate how special the Bible is. But the more I read it, the more I am convinced it is true—not only truthful, but truly the Word of God. Every time I read the Bible, it speaks to me. Even Jesus honored, enjoyed, and often quoted from Scripture—and he was the Son of God!

Let me challenge you with this: Read the Bible. You don't have to start at the beginning and read it straight through. In fact, you'd probably enjoy it more by starting with a book like Psalms, Matthew, Mark, Luke, or John. If you take this challenge, text or email me something the Bible said to you this week.

WEEKLY GRAPPLE CONNECTION
(You can use this as an email template to send to parents)

Grapple Question: Who Came Up With This?
Kids Learn: The Bible Is Inspired by God
Dig Into the Bible: 2 Timothy 3:16-17

Most people would say that reading the Bible is important. But if we checked out our calendars, would it be clear that it's a priority for us?

Here's what 2 Timothy 3:16-17 tells us: "All Scripture is inspired by God and is useful to teach us what is true and to make us realize what is wrong in our lives. It corrects us when we are wrong and teaches us to do what is right. God uses it to prepare and equip his people to do every good work."

Write this passage on a few notecards this week, and put the cards in places you'll see them. Use this passage as a reminder of the importance of studying God's Word. When your kids see this as a priority for you, it will become important to them, too!

- -

LESSON 1

In your Grapple Team, use this guide to grapple with today's question. What is the Bible really about? Who are all these authors? Who put all of it together? How do we know it is really the Word of God?

The Bible has two basic purposes:
1. It tells the story of God's relationship with humanity, and it tells of God's "rescue mission" on our behalf.
2. It's a guidebook to live life the way God designed it.

IN PAIRS

Summarize God's story by answering these questions:

Who are the main characters? _____

Who is the antagonist—the bad guy? _____

What is the conflict? _____

How is the conflict resolved? _____

What happens at the end? _____

Now for the second purpose: How is the Bible like a guidebook?
What are five ways the Bible tells us about how to live life?

1) _____

2) _____

3) _____

4) _____

5) _____

These books were written by people who knew God intimately; they had personal encounters with God. The authors wrote about events, miracles, and truths they had witnessed, experienced, or received.

Read John 21:24-25.

IN PAIRS

Obviously, firsthand knowledge is always better than something heard from a friend who heard it from a friend who heard it from a friend. Discuss how much you trust that the testimonies of John and other writers are accurate. How much of the Bible do you think is from God, and how much is from people?

The books in the Bible are not all the books that were written about God. However, over many centuries, these books became the ones that were considered the most reliable. In other words, if you could have used Google to search "God" back then, these 66 books would have been the first results to show up.

If you were one of those people deciding which books of the Bible to include and which to exclude, how would you make that decision?

_____

_____

Read 2 Timothy 3:16-17.

What does it mean that the Bible is "inspired by God"? How is that different from being written by God?

_____

_____

Read 2 Peter 1:20-21.

What role did the Holy Spirit play in the writing of the Bible? Why is that important?

_____

_____

Read Matthew 5:17.

What role does Jesus play? Based on what Jesus says in this verse, why is it helpful to read the Old Testament, not just the New Testament?

_____

_____

GRAPPLE TEAM REPORTS
With your team, choose one of the options below to report what you discovered.

Option 1: Text It
Write a 160-word text message that you could send to a friend or family member explaining what you learned today.

Option 2: Relay Report
Discuss some of the big ideas you've learned today. Once you're ready to make your presentation to the other team, line up on one side of the room. Run down to the other end of the room and back. When you return, tell about something you learned today. Then the next person in line runs to the end of the room and back, and reports something else. Continue until everyone has participated.

WHO CAME UP WITH THIS?

2 Timothy 3:16
All Scripture is inspired by God and is useful to teach us what is true and to make us realize what is wrong in our lives. It corrects us when we are wrong and teaches us to do what is right.

GRAPPLE CHAT

Chat 1: Discover how many books are in the Old Testament and in the New Testament.

Chat 2: How many books, of any kind, have you read since the beginning of this year?

Chat 3: Find the book of the Bible, other than Genesis, that starts with the words "In the beginning."

Chat 4: What is your favorite book of the Bible, and why?

GRAPPLE CHALLENGE

Read three chapters from a book of the Bible every night this week. Consider reading from like a book like Psalms, Matthew, Mark, Luke, or John.

NOTES:

_____

_____

_____

_____

_____

_____

_____

_____

WORD!!

Isn'th It Justth an Oldth Bookth?
The Point: The Bible Is Alive and Applicable
The Passages: John 1:1-5; Hebrews 4:12-13

GET STARTED
Lesson 2. Isn'th It Justth an Oldth Bookth?

GRAPPLE SCHEDULE

5 MINUTES	HANG TIME
10 MINUTES	GRAPPLE CHAT
10-15 MINUTES	GRAPPLE TIME
20-25 MINUTES	TEAM TIME
10 MINUTES	TEAM REPORTS
5 MINUTES	PRAYER & CHALLENGE

SUPPLIES
Bibles, Grapple DVD, DVD player, music CD, CD player, copy of the Grapple Team Guide for each person, paper, pens or pencils, two baskets or other containers, copies of maps printed from a mapping website

BIBLE BASIS FOR TEACHERS
The Passage: Hebrews 4:12-13
Because we're looking at just two verses of Scripture as our main text, let's take some time and examine the text piece by piece.

- **Alive and powerful.** The author of Hebrews talks about the Word of God being alive. The Bible isn't some dead book; it is alive in people who read it, obey it, and live by it. It is active because it works in people's lives to accomplish God's purpose.

- **Sharper than the sharpest two-edged sword.** A double-edged sword was one of the sharpest implements known to people in New Testament times.

- **Cutting between soul and spirit, between joint and marrow.** God's Word can penetrate deep into our being and show us things hidden inside us.

- **Exposes our innermost thoughts and desires.** God's Word not only judges outward actions that others see, but also the actual motives and attitudes that drive us.

- **He is the one to whom we are accountable.** Once our motives and attitudes are exposed, God's Word holds us accountable to God.

How does this relate to the Grapple Question? Whether or not they trust it, kids who have been raised in the church know what the Bible is, and they know that it's important. However, kids who haven't been exposed to church or Sunday school may conclude that the Bible is just an old book written by old men in an attempt to explain things that science has since been able to explain. Students will grapple with whether or not the Bible is applicable at all for individuals today. Does the Bible make a real difference in our lives, or is the study and application of this old book a waste of time? Kids will learn that God's Word is a guidebook given to us in order to find new life in God.

How does this connect to Jesus? Jesus used Scripture for very real and practical things. Jesus used Scripture to fight temptation (see Matthew 4:4, 7, 10), to make theological points (see Matthew 22:29-30; Luke 19:46), and to point out the fulfillment of prophecy (see Mark 7:6; 9:13). Jesus modeled for us the usefulness of Scripture and its application to himself and his ministry—and it is still relevant for us today.

GRAPPLE HANG TIME: 5 MINUTES
Play music as kids enjoy snacks and friendship, and then play an opening countdown from the Grapple DVD to wrap up Grapple Hang Time.

GRAPPLE CHAT: 10 MINUTES
Have students form pairs; if you have an uneven number of kids, it's OK to have one trio in the mix. Ask each group to chat about two of the four topics below that relate to today's grapple topic. (Answers in parentheses are samples.)

IN PAIRS
Chat 1: Name or find two popular sayings that have their origins in the Bible. (Do to others whatever you would like them to do to you, Matthew 7:12; Turn the other cheek, Matthew 5:39; Do not judge others, and you will not be judged, Matthew 7:1; Ask and you will receive, Matthew 7:8)

Chat 2: Have you ever read a book—besides the Bible—that was written before 1700? before 1800? before 1900?

Chat 3: Find someone in the Bible—other than Jesus—who quoted from Scripture. (Satan, Matthew 4; Peter, Acts 2; Paul, Acts 13)

Chat 4: Does your family own anything that's over 100 years old? If so, tell what it is. If not, tell about some other "old" item your family owns.

GRAPPLE TIME: 10-15 MINUTES
Get Ready: Cue the Grapple DVD to the "The Runaway" clip.

Lead the entire class in the following:
Today we're going to start out with a game of Charades. If your birthday is between January 1 and June 30, go to one side of the room. If your birthday is between July 1 and December 31, go to the opposite side of the room.

If the teams are noticeably uneven, ask a few kids to switch sides. Give each team small pieces of paper and pencils. Have one team quietly brainstorm several well-known TV shows and movies that are at least five years old and write one each on the papers. Have the other team brainstorm several well-known songs that are at least five years old and write them one each on the papers. Give teams a minute or two to do this, and then collect the papers in two containers.

Time's up! Let's play Team Charades now. One team was brainstorming well-known songs. The other team was brainstorming TV shows and movies. I need one person from the music team to draw a slip from the TV-and-movies basket. Work with a teammate to quickly act out something about that show or movie to get your team to guess what it is. Then someone from the other team will draw a song and work with a teammate to act out the song for that team. Remember: no words or sounds! Let's play!

Play several rounds, alternating teams and keeping the action moving fast. You may want to enforce a 30-second time limit to keep things flowing. Make sure different kids are doing the acting for each round.

IN PAIRS
Did you know most of those songs? Do you ever watch any of those TV shows or movies? How difficult would this activity have been if you had been asked to select shows, movies, or songs that were at least 50 years old? What do you like about old music? What do you not like about it? What do you like about old TV shows and movies? What don't you like about them?

TELL ALL
What did you talk about? What are some good things about old stuff? Explain.

Let's watch a video that illustrates how old things can still apply to our lives.

Show the "The Runaway" clip on the Grapple DVD.

The Bible was written a long time ago for people who were extremely different from us here in the 21st century. Can we really learn anything from Jonah or David? Why would anything in the Bible apply to us today? Isn't the Bible just an old book, written by old men, for people who didn't understand modern science and technology? Let's grapple with that.

GRAPPLE TEAM TIME: 20-25 MINUTES

Break into Grapple Teams. Encourage Grapple Team leaders to check in with kids about their week. Grapple Team leaders will facilitate discussion, using the Grapple Team Guide on pages 19-20. Afterward, students will report what they learned.

GRAPPLE TEAM REPORTS: 10 MINUTES

At the end of Grapple Team Time, match Grapple Teams that chose Option 1 with Grapple Teams that chose Option 2 from page 20. Have teams present their reports. (If you have an uneven number of teams, simply form one group of three teams for the presentations. If you have only two Grapple Teams, simply do the presentations one team at a time.)

GRAPPLE PRAYER AND CHALLENGE: 5 MINUTES

Read the Grapple Prayer options. Have the class choose one prayer option that everyone will do. Allow students time to pray about what they discovered. Then close in prayer.

Get Ready: For Option 1, distribute copies of maps printed from a mapping website.

Option 1: Roadmap of Wisdom

Look at a map, and consider all the different roads and highways and streets feature on that map. Pray for God's guidance, wisdom, and direction in your life, and ask God for strength in following the path and plan he has created for you.

Option 2: Prayer Partners

Find a partner to pray with. Talk about troubles you currently face, especially anything connected to today's lesson. Then pray for each other to be able to see your situation from God's perspective.

GRAPPLE CHALLENGE

The Bible is a powerful book that is relevant for all ages. No other book you will ever read has the power to affect you the way the Bible does. Discover the Bible's power for yourself. Read one chapter of the Bible every day and find one thing in that chapter to apply to your life. Let the Bible change your life.

WEEKLY GRAPPLE CONNECTION
(You can use this as an email template to send to parents)

Grapple Question: Isn'th It Justth an Oldth Bookth?
Kids Learn: The Bible Is Alive and Applicable
Dig Into the Bible: Hebrews 4:12-13

Start a family discussion around your dinner table or during a car ride today. Ask each family member to rate, on a scale of 1 to 10 (10 means it's extremely relevant; 1 means it's not relevant at all), how much he or she agrees with this statement: "The Bible is relevant to me today." Give each person a chance to explain his or her rating.

The Bible was written a long time ago, for people who were extremely different from people in the 21st century. Sometimes it seems like the Bible is just an old book, written by old men for people who hadn't yet developed modern science and technology. But the Bible is one powerful book—it is relevant for all ages! Challenge each person in your family to find a way to make the Bible real and alive for them this week. (Some suggestions: Interview a "veteran Christian" to find out what the Bible means to him or her; paraphrase some confusing verses into more readable language; think of one way to live out a meaningful truth from the Bible.) This time next week, check up on one another to see how it's going!

- -

LESSON 2
In your Grapple Team, use this guide to grapple with today's question.

List three things that are more than 100 years old but still very valuable. Discuss in your Grapple Team several reasons why the things you chose are valuable.

Read aloud Hebrews 4:12-13.

IN PAIRS
Tell about a time you…
- found that a verse or an event in the Bible helped you out in a difficult time.
- found good advice in the Bible.
- found comfort in the Bible.
- found something in the Bible that helped you make a decision.
- thought about the Bible during your everyday activities.
- felt like something in the Bible was written exactly for just you.
- found answers to your questions in the Bible.
- felt like you needed to confess something because of what you read in the Bible.
- became a better friend because of something in the Bible.
- changed your actions because of something in the Bible.

How does knowing that God knows everything about you make you feel? Why?

_____

_____

Read aloud John 1:1-5.

In these verses, who is referred to as the Word? Why do you think that is? What do these five verses tell you about Jesus? What do these five verses tell you about the Bible?

IN PAIRS

How has knowing Jesus helped you grow or endure a hardship? Discuss how the Bible has helped you through a difficult time or with a tough decision. Share other examples of how your relationship with Jesus and/or your knowledge of the Bible has applied to your life.

GRAPPLE TEAM REPORTS

With your team, choose one of the options below to report what you discovered.

Option 1: Top 5

Create a Top 5 list of the most important, challenging, or meaningful things you learned today. Be prepared to explain why each item on the list is so important, challenging, or meaningful.

Option 2: Proverb It

Look through the book of Proverbs and find one verse that best connects to what you learned today. If you have enough time, consider finding additional verses.

ISN'TH IT JUSTTH AN OLDTH BOOKTH?

2 Timothy 3:16
All Scripture is inspired by God and is useful to teach us what is true and to make us realize what is wrong in our lives. It corrects us when we are wrong and teaches us to do what is right.

GRAPPLE CHAT
Chat 1: Name or find two popular sayings that have their origins in the Bible.

Chat 2: Have you ever read a book—besides the Bible—that was written before 1700? before 1800? before 1900?

Chat 3: Find someone in the Bible—other than Jesus—who quoted from Scripture.

Chat 4: Does your family own anything that's over 100 years old? If so, tell what it is. If not, tell about some other "old" item your family owns.

GRAPPLE CHALLENGE
Read one chapter of the Bible every day and find one thing in that chapter to apply to your life.

NOTES:

_____

_____

_____

_____

_____

_____

_____

WORD!!

WHY SHOULD I CARE?

WORD!!

Why Should I Care?
The Point: The Bible Equips Us
The Passages: Psalm 119:9-24, 105; Matthew 4:1-11

GET STARTED
Lesson 3. Why Should I Care?

GRAPPLE SCHEDULE

5 MINUTES	HANG TIME
10 MINUTES	GRAPPLE CHAT
10-15 MINUTES	GRAPPLE TIME
20-25 MINUTES	TEAM TIME
10 MINUTES	TEAM REPORTS
5 MINUTES	PRAYER & CHALLENGE

SUPPLIES
Bibles, Grapple DVD, DVD player, music CD, CD player, copy of the Grapple Team Guide for each person, paper, pens or pencils, small pieces of masking tape, markers

BIBLE BASIS FOR TEACHERS
The Passage: Psalm 119:9-24
Psalm 119 is the longest of all the 150 psalms. It is organized into 22 separate sections, one section for each letter in the Hebrew alphabet. Each section focuses on the essential importance of God's Word. Certain sections focus on God's teachings, others center on God's commandments, and still other sections appeal to the promises found in God's Word. This structure helps worshippers focus on the specifics of God's law and teaching, and it offers readers a guide to meditating on God's Word in a meaningful way.

This week's passage includes the second and third sections of Psalm 119. Like most of this psalm, these two sections not only focus on the importance of God's Word, but also allude to the benefits that come along with knowing the living Word of God.

How does this relate to the Grapple Question? Kids are told that the Bible is useful and that by reading it they can receive guidance and insight into their daily lives. But how many kids truly believe that the Bible actually has something valuable to offer them? For some, the Bible is just an old book that doesn't offer anything useful. They may even wonder why anyone should care about what lies within the pages of God's Word. For this lesson, students will grapple with whether or not the Bible is effective. Some people think that if they've read the

Bible once, they've read it enough. They may say something like, "I know how it ends—why should I read it again?" as if the Bible were the latest novel by a famous author. This lesson will help kids grapple with this very issue and come to a better understanding of how God's Word truly equips those who take it seriously.

How does this connect to Jesus? Students will begin to see that Jesus used the Bible as a tool. When he was tempted in the wilderness, he used the Bible to defeat the devil's designs (see Matthew 4:1-11). When he was on the cross, he used the Bible as a teaching tool and as a way to express significant spiritual events (see Matthew 27:46 and Psalm 22). Jesus consistently used the Bible to equip his own spiritual growth and his ministry. By looking to Jesus as our model and following him down the path of discipleship, we can experience the Bible as a powerful tool to equip us in growth and ministry.

GRAPPLE HANG TIME: 5 MINUTES
Play music as kids enjoy snacks and friendship, and then play an opening countdown from the Grapple DVD to wrap up Grapple Hang Time.

GRAPPLE CHAT: 10 MINUTES
Have students form pairs; if you have an uneven number of kids, it's OK to have one trio in the mix. Ask each group to chat about two of the four topics below that relate to today's grapple topic. (Answers in parentheses are samples.)

IN PAIRS
Chat 1: Find out what Jesus told the disciples to pack for their first missionary journey. (Nothing, Luke 9:3)

Chat 2: If you were stranded on a desert island, what three supplies would you want in your backpack, and why?

Chat 3: Discover who appeared to Jesus when he took Peter, James, and John up a mountain. (Moses and Elijah, Mark 9:2-13)

Chat 4: What is the longest hike you ever went on, and what were some of the challenges you encountered along the way? What was the highlight of the hike for you?

GRAPPLE TIME: 10-15 MINUTES
Get Ready: Cue the Grapple DVD to the "Tools" clip.

Lead the entire class in the following:
Have kids form teams, and give teams paper and pens or pencils.

Work together to list equipment that would help these people when they encountered their foes. Be creative!

- A young shepherd boy facing a strong giant in battle
- A man facing a den of hungry lions
- A small army facing an armed, walled city
- A shepherd facing the king of Egypt
- Jesus facing Satan in the desert

Then look in the Bible for Paul's list of spiritual armor. (Ephesians 6)

IN PAIRS
Share a story about a time you really wished you had some equipment to make your experience or trial easier.

TELL ALL
Share your answers. How is the Bible like necessary equipment, good directions, or a helpful map?

Let's watch a video to learn more about the Bible as a map, a tool, or a GPS.

Show the "Tools" clip on the Grapple DVD.

What's the big deal about the Bible? Why do some people spend so much time and energy worrying about what the Bible says? The Bible can't provide me with food and clothing, can it? The Bible can't protect me from harm, can it? The Bible can't help me find friends or help me pass my math test, can it? Why should I even care? Let's grapple with that.

GRAPPLE TEAM TIME: 20-25 MINUTES
Break into Grapple Teams. Encourage Grapple Team leaders to check in with kids about their week. Grapple Team leaders will facilitate discussion, using the Grapple Team Guide on pages 28-30. Afterward, students will report what they learned.

GRAPPLE TEAM REPORTS: 10 MINUTES
At the end of Grapple Team Time, match Grapple Teams that chose Option 1 with Grapple Teams that chose Option 2 from page 30. Have teams present their reports. (If you have an uneven number of teams, simply form one group of three teams for the presentations. If you have only two Grapple Teams, simply do the presentations one team at a time.)

GRAPPLE PRAYER AND CHALLENGE: 5 MINUTES
Read the Grapple Prayer options. Have the class choose one prayer option that everyone will do. Allow students time to pray about what they discovered. Then close in prayer.

Get Ready: for Option 1, distribute markers and small pieces of masking tape.

Option 1: Sticky Situations

Write one of your weaknesses on a small piece of masking tape. Put the tape on your arm, leg, or face. Then pray, asking God to be strong in your weakness. Ask God to speak up for you as your enemy tries to hurt you.

Option 2: Still Small Voice

Close your eyes and think about one difficult thing you're currently going through. Ask God to show you where he is in this situation. After a period of reflective silence, ask God what he is trying to say to you through this circumstance. Write down any thoughts or ideas that come to mind.

GRAPPLE CHALLENGE

Some people stink at asking for directions. They attempt to feel their way to a desired destination. Sometimes it works. Sometimes it gets them totally lost. Our spiritual journey can be similar to that—we hate asking God for directions. We don't think to look at the map—God's Word—for instruction. We mostly feel our way through and do the best we can. I've learned that in life it is better to ask for directions—and that includes our journey with God. Next time you need help, instead of trying to feel your way through, go to God instead. Read the Bible and search for God's direction. You'll achieve a better result.

WEEKLY GRAPPLE CONNECTION
(You can use this as an email template to send to parents)

Grapple Question: Why Should I Care?
Kids Learn: The Bible Equips Us
Dig Into the Bible: Psalm 119:9-24

Does your family struggle to see the point of reading the Bible? Make things a little more interesting this week by challenging everyone to a friendly competition. Invite family members to choose a memorable event from their week and find a Scripture passage that's relevant to that event. Then treat everyone to a special dessert as you all share what you found.

- -

LESSON 3

In your Grapple Team, use this guide to grapple with today's question.

How to escape from an anaconda:

1. Do not run. The snake is faster than you are.
2. Lie flat on the ground, place your arms tightly against your sides, and press your legs against one another.
3. Tuck in your chin.
4. The snake will begin to nudge and crawl over your body.
5. Do not panic.
6. The snake will begin to swallow you from the feet end. Permit the snake to swallow your feet and ankles. Do not panic!
7. The snake will now begin to suck your legs into its body. You must lie perfectly still. This will take a long time.
8. When it has reached your knees slowly reach down, take your knife and slide it into the snake's mouth between the edge of its mouth and your leg. Suddenly rip upwards, severing the snake's head.
9. Be sure you have a knife.
10. Be sure the knife is sharp.
(It's a joke, of course!)

IN PAIRS

What might happen if these instructions were real and you followed steps 1 through 7 before reading steps 8, 9, and 10? In what ways do you think the Bible could be a survival handbook?

Read Matthew 4:1-11.

Jesus found himself in a worst-case scenario. He had been in the wilderness fasting (going without food) for 40 days when Satan appeared and tempted him. What were the three temptations?

1) _____

2) _____

3) _____

In each instance, Jesus defended himself from Satan's attacks by using Scripture. What if he hadn't known the verses? How is Jesus' use of Scripture like the anaconda example you read earlier? How is it NOT like the anaconda example?

IN PAIRS

The Bible is a book, a large collection of events and teachings and other writings. But in what ways is it also a weapon? Think of a time that knowing Scripture helped you or would have helped you. Share the story with your partner.

Read Psalm 119:9-24.

Using these verses, find three ways God's Word can help you be prepared to fight off temptation and make right choices about how to live.

1) _____

2) _____

3) _____

GRAPPLE TEAM REPORTS
With your team, choose one of the options below to report what you discovered.

Option 1: Instant Object Lesson
Use whatever you can find around you to create some instant object lessons that explain what you learned today. Get creative!

Option 2: New Perspective
Talk about how today's lesson has changed your perspective on the Bible. And then get a new physical perspective: Stand on a table, stand on your head, stretch out on the floor—whatever you want! Hold that position as one member of your team explains how today's lesson has provided a new perspective. Do a "test run" as a team before making your presentation to the other team.

WHY SHOULD I CARE?

2 Timothy 3:16
All Scripture is inspired by God and is useful to teach us what is true and to make us realize what is wrong in our lives. It corrects us when we are wrong and teaches us to do what is right.

GRAPPLE CHAT
Chat 1: Find out what Jeus told the disciples to pack for their first missionary journey.

Chat 2: If you were stranded on a desert island, what three supplies would you want in your backpack, and why?

Chat 3: Discover who appeared to Jesus when he took Peter, James, and John up a mountain.

Chat 4: What is the longest hike you ever went on, and what were some of the challenges you encountered along the way? What was the highlight of the hike for you?

GRAPPLE CHALLENGE
Before making an important decision this week, spend some time reading God's Word for direction and guidance.

NOTES:

_____

_____

_____

_____

_____

_____

_____

WORD!!

WILL THERE BE A TEST?

WORD!!

Will There Be a Test?
The Point: Studying the Bible Helps Us Grow
The Passages: Psalm 119:81-112; Matthew 21:12-17; 1 John 2:14

GET STARTED
Lesson 4. Will There Be a Test?

GRAPPLE SCHEDULE

5 MINUTES	HANG TIME
10 MINUTES	GRAPPLE CHAT
10-15 MINUTES	GRAPPLE TIME
20-25 MINUTES	TEAM TIME
10 MINUTES	TEAM REPORTS
5 MINUTES	PRAYER & CHALLENGE

SUPPLIES
Bibles, Grapple DVD, DVD player, music CD, CD player, copy of the Grapple Team Guide for each person, paper, pens or pencils

BIBLE BASIS FOR TEACHERS
The Passage: Psalm 119:81-112
Psalm 119 doesn't exactly teach us how to study the Bible, but it definitely expresses the importance of God's Word and the importance of spending time with it. This passage in particular emphasizes the importance of not only reading Scripture but also knowing it. True knowledge of God's Word comes through constant, faithful study and meditation focused on God's Word.

How does this relate to the Grapple Question? Kids often wonder why we are instructed or encouraged to study the Bible. From the beginning of their education, kids are tested to determine how well they're learning their particular school's curriculum. By the time students reach junior high, grades and scores become the focus. Content is perceived as being valuable only if it comes with a test. Kids are encouraged to read the Bible, but because there isn't a written test over the knowledge and wisdom they obtain from it, teenagers often don't realize the inherent value of studying Scripture. For this lesson, students will grapple with whether or not there is value and importance in studying the Bible.

How does this connect to Jesus? By the time Jesus was 12 years old, he amazed the religious teachers with his understanding of Scripture (see Luke 2:47). It is also apparent that Jesus knew Scripture very well, that he had spent his entire life studying the Word of God.

In order to follow Jesus and grow as disciples of Jesus, we are called to do the same—to study the Word of God in order to grow in wisdom, in understanding, and in relationship with God.

GRAPPLE HANG TIME: 5 MINUTES
Play music as kids enjoy snacks and friendship, and then play an opening countdown from the Grapple DVD to wrap up Grapple Hang Time.

GRAPPLE CHAT: 10 MINUTES
Have students form pairs; if you have an uneven number of kids, it's OK to have one trio in the mix. Ask each group to chat about two of the four topics below that relate to today's grapple topic. (Answers in parentheses are samples.)

IN PAIRS
Chat 1: Find someone in the Bible—other than Jesus—who taught others about God's Word. (Moses, Exodus 20; Philip, Acts 8)

Chat 2: How much taller have you grown in just the past year? past two years? Did you experience quick, fast growth, or was it slower and almost unnoticeable at the time?

Chat 3: Discover one example in the Bible of someone talking about growing and harvesting plants. (Joseph's dream, Genesis 37; Ruth gleaning in the fields, Ruth 2; the parable of the seeds, Matthew 13; the parable of the vineyard workers, Matthew 20)

Chat 4: How many live houseplants do you have at home? Do your parents give you any responsibility for caring for these plants? Why or why not?

GRAPPLE TIME: 10-15 MINUTES
Get Ready: Cue the Grapple DVD to the "No Tests" clip.

Lead the entire class in the following:
Everybody stand up and spread out! We're looking a little tired today, so I think we should start with some calisthenics. Ready? Let's go!

Lead the class in some jumping jacks, toe touches, windmills, lunges, and maybe even squats, sit-ups, or push-ups if you're feeling up to it. Keep up a banter about working your muscles—your biceps and triceps, rock-hard abs, and glutes. After a few minutes, let kids sit down.

Good job, everyone! What a great workout!

TELL ALL
What else, besides exercise, do we need in order to grow healthy and strong?

IN PAIRS

What do most organic things need in order to grow? What's an example from your own life of something that died because it didn't get what it needed to grow? How did that experience change you, if at all?

TELL ALL

What are some ways people grow other than physically? What are some things we need in order to grow in those ways? What happens if we don't get those things or do those things?

Let's watch a video to learn more about what it takes to grow spiritually.

Show the "No Tests" clip on the Grapple DVD.

What makes something worth learning about? Is the information in the Bible really a big deal? Is it really important to learn all the details in the Bible? Does it really matter if we read Leviticus or not? If no one is going to test us on the information, why should we care about the Bible? Let's grapple with that.

GRAPPLE TEAM TIME: 20-25 MINUTES

Break into Grapple Teams. Encourage Grapple Team leaders to check in with kids about their week. Grapple Team leaders will facilitate discussion, using the Grapple Team Guide on pages 38-40. Afterward, students will report what they learned.

GRAPPLE TEAM REPORTS: 10 MINUTES

At the end of Grapple Team Time, match Grapple Teams that chose Option 1 with Grapple Teams that chose Option 2 from page 40. Have teams present their reports. (If you have an uneven number of teams, simply form one group of three teams for the presentations. If you have only two Grapple Teams, simply do the presentations one team at a time.)

GRAPPLE PRAYER AND CHALLENGE: 5 MINUTES

Read the Grapple Prayer options. Have the class choose one prayer option that everyone will do. Allow students time to pray about what they discovered. Then close in prayer.

Get Ready: for Option 1, distribute sheets of paper and make sure students have pens or pencils.

Option 1: Prayer Pile

Get in a circle with the rest of your group. Write a prayer to God. Then crumple up the paper with the prayer on it and make a pile of crumpled papers in the middle of the circle. Choose one crumpled prayer from the pile. Silently pray the words written on the paper, and then ask God to answer the prayer for the person who wrote it.

Option 2: You Are; I Am

Find a partner to pray with. God gave us the Bible so we could know him and so we could know who we really are. Take turns each praying a one-sentence prayer that starts, "God, you are…." Then take turns each praying a one-sentence prayer that starts with the words: "Because of your love for me, God, I am…."

GRAPPLE CHALLENGE

Studying the Bible helps us grow. Just as our bodies need healthy food and exercise to grow properly and our brains need new information and stimulation to grow, our spirits need to be fed from God's Word to grow. Feed yourself from God's Word, the Bible. Study one psalm this week, really digging in. Focus on what God is saying to you in that psalm this week.

WEEKLY GRAPPLE CONNECTION
(You can use this as an email template to send to parents)

Grapple Question: Will There Be a Test?
Kids Learn: Studying the Bible Helps Us Grow
Dig Into the Bible: Psalm 119:81-112

If your teenager could eat anything he or she wanted this week, what do you think that meal plan would look like? Would there be a healthy balance of vegetables and protein—or a bag of Doritos® and a can of Mountain Dew®?

Just as our bodies need healthy food and exercise to grow properly, our souls need to be fed from God's Word in order to grow. One night this week, feed your family both physically and spiritually. As you eat together, take the opportunity to also read a favorite chapter of the Bible together (if you're not sure where to start, try Romans 12 or 1 Corinthians 13). You'll not only be growing closer together as a family, you'll also be building deeper relationships with God!

- -

LESSON 4

In your Grapple Team, use this guide to grapple with today's question.

Read aloud Psalm 119:81-112.

IN PAIRS

Pay particular attention to Psalm 119:89-104. What reasons do these verses offer for reading, studying, memorizing, or meditating on God's Word? How have you used the Bible to grow in your relationship with God?

89-91: _____

_____

92-93: _____

_____

94-96: _____

_____

97-99: _____

_____

100-102: _____

_____

103-104: _____

_____

Read aloud 1 John 2:14.

How can knowing the Word of God help you win your battle against the evil one? What steps can you take to keep the Bible alive in your heart?

_____

_____

Read aloud Matthew 21:12-17.

This passage shows how Jesus used Scripture to accuse the money changers of disobeying God. He also used Scripture to defend the children because they were praising God for sending Jesus. Is it OK to use the Bible to accuse someone? to defend someone?

Why or why not?

_____

_____

GRAPPLE TEAM REPORTS

With your team, choose one of the options below to report what you discovered.

Option 1: Knowit Poets!

Write a poem or a rap about what you learned today, making every sentence contain the word *grow*.

Option 2: ABCs

Write the ABCs of what you learned today: a statement that starts with an A, a statement that starts with a B, and so on. Try to go as far into the alphabet as you can—even all the way to Z.

WILL THERE BE A TEST?

2 Timothy 3:16
All Scripture is inspired by God and is useful to teach us what is true and to make us realize what is wrong in our lives. It corrects us when we are wrong and teaches us to do what is right.

GRAPPLE CHAT

Chat 1: Find someone in the Bible—other than Jesus—who taught others about God's Word.

Chat 2: How much taller have you grown in just the past year? past two years? Did you experience quick, fast growth, or was it slower and almost unnoticeable at the time?

Chat 3: Discover one example in the Bible of someone talking about growing and harvesting plants.

Chat 4: How many live houseplants do you have at home? Do your parents give you any responsibility for caring for these plants? Why or why not?

GRAPPLE CHALLENGE

Read one psalm this week, and write down two ways that the psalm spoke to you.

NOTES:

_____

_____

_____

_____

_____

_____

_____

_____

IT'S MY LIFE

WHO DO I TELL?

IT'S MY LIFE

Who Do I Tell?
The Point: Know My Sphere of Influence
The Passages: Matthew 28:18-20; Acts 1:1-8

GET STARTED
Lesson 5. Who Do I Tell?

GRAPPLE SCHEDULE

5 MINUTES	HANG TIME
10 MINUTES	GRAPPLE CHAT
10-15 MINUTES	GRAPPLE TIME
20-25 MINUTES	TEAM TIME
10 MINUTES	TEAM REPORTS
5 MINUTES	PRAYER & CHALLENGE

SUPPLIES
Bibles, Grapple DVD, DVD player, music CD, CD player, copy of the Grapple Team Guide for each person, paper, pens or pencils

BIBLE BASIS FOR TEACHERS
The Passage: Acts 1:1-8
As we look at this passage, we see Jesus talking about the power his followers would receive—not the political power they perhaps were hoping for, but something actually much better: the power of the Holy Spirit. Jesus' disciples had seen him do mighty things by the power of the Holy Spirit, and now he was promising that power to them. With it, he was giving them the privilege of telling others about him.

The last recorded words Jesus spoke before ascending to heaven describe the process by which the early church would grow. The news about Christ spread through Jerusalem, then to Judea and Samaria, and then to the rest of the known world. And now we have the privilege of taking the message of Jesus to our world today.

How does this relate to the Grapple Question? When some Christian adults hear about sharing Jesus with other people, they freeze in fear, and early adolescents aren't any different. It can be pretty scary to go out there and talk about Jesus with just anyone. For this lesson, students will discuss their spheres of influence. They'll grapple with whether or not they have to tell complete strangers about Jesus, or just their closest friends and family.

It's our hope that kids will learn to become more comfortable sharing Jesus with others because they'll learn that they can slowly increase their sphere of influence at a comfortable pace.

How does this connect to Jesus? Jesus told the disciples how to share his story with others. They were to start where they were, in Jerusalem, and spread the message outward. The model Jesus used is the same model we are to use today. Begin by telling your story to your closest friends and family. Then expand outward by sharing with neighbors and acquaintances. Continue by sharing with total strangers or even enemies. It would be absurd to begin sharing the good news with strangers if your best friend still hasn't heard the message. By knowing our sphere of influence, we can definitely have a positive impact on the world in the name of Jesus.

GRAPPLE HANG TIME: 5 MINUTES
Play music as kids enjoy snacks and friendship, and then play an opening countdown from the Grapple DVD to wrap up Grapple Hang Time.

GRAPPLE CHAT: 10 MINUTES
Have students form pairs; if you have an uneven number of kids, it's OK to have one trio in the mix. Ask each group to chat about two of the four topics below that relate to today's grapple topic. (Answers in parentheses are samples.)

IN PAIRS
Chat 1: Find out what Isaiah refers to as "good news." (Peace, salvation, and a radical change in the status quo, Isaiah 52:7 and 61:1)

Chat 2: What are the names of the last three people you've had a conversation with, and what did you discuss?

Chat 3: Discover what Jesus tells his followers to do near the end of Mark's Gospel. (Go into the world and preach the good news, Mark 16:15)

Chat 4: Give three examples of what you would consider good news, and explain why each would be good news.

GRAPPLE TIME: 10-15 MINUTES
Get Ready: Cue the Grapple DVD to the "One Step at a Time" clip.

Lead the entire class in the following:

Think of something you've been really excited about in the last month: a movie you saw, a new store at the mall, the best video game you've played, a new song for your MP3 player, the sport you play, and so on. When I say "Go!" you'll have two minutes to convince as many people in the room as you can to try that thing. Questions? Pause. Go!

IN PAIRS

How did you decide what to talk about? How did you decide who to tell? Did you prefer talking or listening? Why? Describe this activity in one or two words—such as *easy, difficult, fun, frustrating*—and explain your word choice.

TELL ALL

What did you hear about that you'd now like to try? What convinced you? What didn't convince you, and why? How is this activity similar to telling others about Jesus?

Show the "One Step at a Time" clip on the Grapple DVD.

Evangelism doesn't have to mean using tricked-out talking techniques on strategically selected people. It can be as natural as talking with anyone God puts in your path about something you're excited about: Jesus! Let's grapple with the question of who we should tell about Jesus.

GRAPPLE TEAM TIME: 20-25 MINUTES

Break into Grapple Teams. Encourage Grapple Team leaders to check in with kids about their week. Grapple Team leaders will facilitate discussion, using the Grapple Team Guide on pages 48-50. Afterward, students will report what they learned.

GRAPPLE TEAM REPORTS: 10 MINUTES

At the end of Grapple Team Time, match Grapple Teams that chose Option 1 with Grapple Teams that chose Option 2 from page 50. Have teams present their reports. (If you have an uneven number of teams, simply form one group of three teams for the presentations. If you have only two Grapple Teams, simply do the presentations one team at a time.)

GRAPPLE PRAYER AND CHALLENGE: 5 MINUTES

Read the Grapple Prayer options. Have the class choose one prayer option that everyone will do. Allow students time to pray about what they discovered. Then close in prayer.

Option 1: Power Prayers

Clench your fists tight as you imagine using all your power to maintain control over all the different areas of your life. Talk with God, asking for his powerful perspective, and gradually unclench your fists as you give God control. With your hands open and empty, ask God to fill you with his empowering, life-giving Spirit.

Option 2: Quiet Prayers

Spread out around the room, and get comfortable so you won't be distracted by others. Psalm 143:10 begins with, "Teach me to do your will." Pray that simple phrase over and over, slowly and quietly, and listen for what the Holy Spirit wants to teach you today. Write down any thoughts or ideas that come to mind as you listen.

GRAPPLE CHALLENGE

The good news of Jesus is that God loves us so much that Jesus died to save us from our sins. The good news of evangelism is that we have the very best, most important message to share with the whole world and that we don't do it alone. The Holy Spirit goes with us, guiding us, even giving us the words to say. This week, pray quietly for the people you see throughout your day, asking the Spirit to guide you to the right people at the right time so you can tell them about the Jesus who loves them more than they will ever know.

WEEKLY GRAPPLE CONNECTION
(You can use this as an email template to send to parents)

Grapple Question: Who Do I Tell?
Kids Learn: Know My Sphere of Influence
Dig Into the Bible: Acts 1:1-8

Sometimes people think of evangelism as a special outreach event at church or an international mission trip. But you come in contact with dozens of people each day at work, at the store, and at the coffee shop. Where does evangelism fit into those relationships?

Discuss with your child how each of you feels about talking to others about Jesus. Is it easier if it's a close friend, or a stranger you probably won't see again? What environments feel more or less comfortable for bringing up that topic? Take this challenge together: For one day, pray quietly for every person you see. Ask the Spirit to guide you to the right people at the right time so you can tell them about the Jesus who loves them more than they will ever know. Follow up the next day to see how this challenge impacted the way you look at sharing your faith.

- -

LESSON 5

In your Grapple Team, use this guide to grapple with today's question.

Share with your team what your favorite thing to talk about is and why it's your favorite.

IN PAIRS

Have you ever convinced someone to try out one of your favorite things? How did you do it? Why did that person agree to try it? What can you learn from that experience that applies to the way you tell others about Jesus?

Read Acts 1:1-8.

Why do you think Jesus spent his last days on earth teaching his followers about the Holy Spirit and God's kingdom and proving that he really was alive? How might Jesus' focus on these truths impact what you tell people about him?

_____

_____

Jesus said his followers would spread the good news in Jerusalem, Judea, Samaria, and around the world. Let's think about that in our own surroundings. Think of individuals or groups of people who are really close to you—like friends or family—who need to know Jesus. Now think of people you don't know very well but could speak to about Jesus. Now think of people you may be uncomfortable speaking to about Jesus. Finally think of a place you would like to influence by sharing about Jesus with the people who live in that place.

How could you affect the people you know and those you come into contact with for Jesus? Are there other people or places God might want you to be involved with?

_____

_____

Take it to the next level. Individually, think about people with whom God might be calling you to share the good news. Keep in mind the groups or places you just listed.

People you know: _____

_____

People you don't know well but have contact with: _____

_____

People you're uncomfortable with or don't like: _____

_____

People around the world: _____

_____

IN PAIRS

How do you feel as you look at your list: overwhelmed, scared, excited, challenged, hopeful? What steps could you take to overcome any insecurities and embrace God's calling in your life to share Jesus with others?

Read Matthew 28:18-20.

Based on this passage, what do you think Jesus is asking you to do now? What comfort can you take from his promise in verse 20?

_____

_____

GRAPPLE TEAM REPORTS

With your team, choose one of the options below to report what you discovered.

Option 1: Condense It

If you had to summarize today's lesson in only five words, what would they be? As a team, choose the words carefully, and be prepared to explain why you chose them.

Option 2: Preach It; Practice It

Create a short instruction manual titled "Practice What You Preach." Come up with at least 10 ways everyone can put today's lesson into practice this next week.

WHO DO I TELL?

Acts 1:8

"But you will receive power when the Holy Spirit comes upon you. And you will be my witnesses, telling people about me everywhere—in Jerusalem, throughout Judea, in Samaria, and to the ends of the earth."

GRAPPLE CHAT

Chat 1: Find out what Isaiah refers to as "good news."

Chat 2: What are the names of the last three people you've had a conversation with, and what did you discuss?

Chat 3: Discover what Jesus tells his followers to do near the end of Mark's Gospel.

Chat 4: Give three examples of what you would consider good news, and explain why each would be good news.

GRAPPLE CHALLENGE

This week pray specifically for two people you know. Pray that God will empower you to share Jesus with them.

NOTES:

_____

_____

_____

_____

_____

_____

_____

_____

IT'S MY LIFE

WHAT MATTERS?

IT'S MY LIFE

What Matters?
The Point: Tell God's Story
**The Passages: John 1:1-18; 3:16; 14:6; Romans 3:23; 5:8; 6:23; 10:9;
1 John 1:8-9**

GET STARTED
Lesson 6. What Matters?

GRAPPLE SCHEDULE

5 MINUTES	HANG TIME
10 MINUTES	GRAPPLE CHAT
10-15 MINUTES	GRAPPLE TIME
20-25 MINUTES	TEAM TIME
10 MINUTES	TEAM REPORTS
5 MINUTES	PRAYER & CHALLENGE

SUPPLIES
Bibles, Grapple DVD, DVD player, music CD, CD player, copy of the Grapple
Team Guide for each person, paper, pens or pencils, bull's-eye, modeling dough
or clay

BIBLE BASIS FOR TEACHERS
The Passage: John 1:1-18
The first sentence of the book of John recalls Genesis 1:1. In this first section
of his Gospel, John outlines the topic he explores throughout the entire book: The
Word—Jesus—is human, is divine, and came to provide salvation for all
who elieve.

In emphasizing that Jesus is God, John attests in verse 3 that Jesus was active in
the Creation. Though Jesus, the God-man, was physically born at a point in time,
he exists eternally as God. John had no doubt about Jesus' divinity.

Despite John's certainty, there were people who disbelieved Jesus. Astonishingly,
they rejected Jesus—their creator. Even so, to those who accepted and believed
in him, he offered "the right to become children of God" just for receiving and
believing in him. What an amazing and merciful God!

In verse 14, John attests to what may be the single hardest idea for his readers to
accept. The Word—God himself—became a human being, with all the limitations,
struggles, and temptations we face. However, in becoming flesh, Jesus did not
cease to be God. Jesus was fully God and fully human, and through his life,
death, and resurrection on earth, he "revealed God to us." God has done it all for
us. All we need to do is believe.

How does this relate to the Grapple Question? When it comes to sharing Jesus with others, many times people freeze up because they don't know the essentials of the gospel message. They may think that they can talk about God for a while, but they're afraid they might miss an important part of the story. This lesson will help kids grasp the essentials—what matters—when it comes to the gospel. Students will discuss how they can include the essential gospel message in their own personal stories.

How does this connect to Jesus? Jesus is what matters. A personal story without Jesus is just a story, and it won't help bring someone closer to a relationship with Jesus. It is essential to include the message of Jesus when we share our stories with others. The fact that God loved us so much that he sacrificed his only Son so we can be forgiven and can have a relationship with him—that's awesome news! That's what matters!

GRAPPLE HANG TIME: 5 MINUTES
Play music as kids enjoy snacks and friendship, and then play an opening countdown from the Grapple DVD to wrap up Grapple Hang Time.

GRAPPLE CHAT: 10 MINUTES
Have students form pairs; if you have an uneven number of kids, it's OK to have one trio in the mix. Ask each group to chat about two of the four topics below that relate to today's grapple topic. (Answers in parentheses are samples.)

IN PAIRS
Chat 1: Find two things that Jesus considered important. (Relationships, John 1:35-42; prayer, Matthew 26:36-46)

Chat 2: What topic do you love to talk about most, and why?

Chat 3: Find a verse that explains the importance of having a relationship with Jesus. (John 3:16; John 14:6; Romans 6:23)

Chat 4: What two possessions matter to you most, and why?

GRAPPLE TIME: 10-15 MINUTES
Get Ready: Cue the Grapple DVD to the "What Matters" clip.

Lead the entire class in the following:

I hope you are all prepared to talk today. Find a partner near you, and decide who will be the talker first. I'll name a topic. If you're the first talker, you'll talk to your partner nonstop for 30 seconds, saying whatever you want about the topic—your opinion, things you've heard, or anything you think of about the topic. Then I'll read the next topic, and your partner will have a turn to talk.

Pause for 30 seconds after you read each topic.
- Your favorite movie
- The last student election at your school
- Different ways chocolate is used in food
- What you appreciate about your best friend
- The difference between English and chemistry
- A story that was recently in the news

TELL ALL
What made certain topics easier to talk about? Did you think what you were saying was meaningful to the other person? How could you have been more prepared to talk about these topics?

IN PAIRS
What are some other topics that are difficult for you to discuss with others? On a scale from 1 (not at all) to 10 (totally), how prepared do you feel to share your faith with others? Why did you choose this number? What would it take to move up one number on the scale?

Show the "What Matters" clip on the Grapple DVD.

So you want to tell someone about your friendship with Jesus. You know it's important to tell your personal story—how knowing God has changed your life. But beyond that, what are the important points to share? What matters? Let's grapple with that!

GRAPPLE TEAM TIME: 20-25 MINUTES
Break into Grapple Teams. Encourage Grapple Team leaders to check in with kids about their week. Grapple Team leaders will facilitate discussion, using the Grapple Team Guide on pages 59-61. Afterward, kids will report what they learned.

GRAPPLE TEAM REPORTS: 10 MINUTES
At the end of Grapple Team Time, match Grapple Teams that chose Option 1 with Grapple Teams that chose Option 2 from page 61. Have teams present their reports. (If you have an uneven number of teams, simply form one group of three teams for the presentations. If you have only two Grapple Teams, simply do the presentations one team at a time.)

GRAPPLE PRAYER AND CHALLENGE: 5 MINUTES
Read the Grapple Prayer options. Have the class choose one prayer option that everyone will do. Allow kids time to pray about what they discovered. Then close in prayer.

Get Ready: For Option 1, affix the bull's-eye to the far wall, and distribute paper to students.

Option 1: Marksman, Markswoman

Make paper airplanes, and take turns throwing the airplanes at the bull's-eye. Walk to wherever your airplane lands and pray to God about one way you miss the mark in your life. Relate what you say to what you learned today.

Option 2: Psalms That Pray

Get comfortable, preferably sitting apart from each other. Look through the book of Psalms and find a psalm that connects with a situation you're facing right now. Read the psalm quietly as a prayer to God.

GRAPPLE CHALLENGE

It's important to be prepared to talk about your faith in Jesus with a friend, neighbor, or family member. You already know it's important to share your personal story about how God has changed your life. But what you say also matters: It matters that we have all sinned. It matters that we don't deserve a relationship with God—but when Jesus died on the cross, he made that relationship possible. This week, share what matters with at least one person. You could make an eternal difference in that person's life, just by having the courage to talk about the important stuff.

WEEKLY GRAPPLE CONNECTION
(You can use this as an email template to send to parents)

Grapple Question: What Matters?
Kids Learn: Tell God's Story
Dig Into the Bible: John 1:1-18

You and your child probably know it's important to share your personal stories about how God has changed your lives. But it also matters what you say: It matters that we have all sinned. It matters that we don't deserve a relationship with God—but Jesus changed all of that by dying for our sins.

Sit down as a family and make a list of some key verses that reveal important information about Jesus and how to have a friendship with him. Try these for starters, but also write down verses that have been important to your personal faith:

- Romans 3:23
- Romans 5:8
- Romans 6:23
- Romans 10:9
- John 3:16
- John 14:6

Give each family member an index card to write down these important verses. Keep the cards handy so you'll have them when you see opportunities to share your faith.

LESSON 6

In your Grapple Team, use this guide to grapple with today's question.

When you're sharing your faith, what are the most important points to talk about? How can you be prepared to talk about your friendship with Jesus?

Read John 1:1-18.

IN PAIRS

Think about what "the Word" means in verses 1 through 5. Who or what is the Word? Why is it important that the Word existed in the beginning? What does it mean to you that the Word is God? Is the Word important to your life right now? In the box below, draw what you think of when you read about the Word. Show your drawing to your partner, and explain what you think the Word is.

In the left column below are verses that people often refer to when talking about their faith. Read each verse, and then write in the column to the right what this verse says about what matters about God. The first one is done as an example.

John 3:16	God loves us so much that Jesus died for us.

John 14:6	
Romans 3:23	
Romans 6:23	
Romans 5:8	
Romans 10:9	
1 John 1:8-9	

IN PAIRS

Why is it important to be prepared to share your faith? According to the passages you read today, what matters most when you're sharing your faith?

Take some time to reflect about what matters to God. What does God want you to share with others? Use a separate sheet of paper, and write some notes or paragraphs about what you would say if a friend asked you about your relationship with Jesus.

GRAPPLE TEAM REPORTS

With your team, choose one of the options below to report what you discovered.

Get Ready: For Option 2, distribute modeling dough or clay.

Option 1: Top 5

Create a Top 5 list of the most important, challenging, or meaningful things you learned today. Be prepared to explain why each item on the list is so important, challenging, or meaningful.

Option 2: Sculpt It

Take some modeling dough or clay, and sculpt objects that explain or reveal what you discovered today. Be prepared to interpret your artwork in case you tend to create abstract art!

WHAT MATTERS?

Acts 1:8
"But you will receive power when the Holy Spirit comes upon you. And you will be my witnesses, telling people about me everywhere—in Jerusalem, throughout Judea, in Samaria, and to the ends of the earth."

GRAPPLE CHAT
Chat 1: Find two things that Jesus considered important.

Chat 2: What topic do you love to talk about most, and why?

Chat 3: Find a verse that explains the importance of having a relationship with Jesus.

Chat 4: What two possessions matter to you most, and why?

GRAPPLE CHALLENGE
This week, have a conversation with a friend and share what matters—that we all sin, we'll all die, Jesus died for us, and we're saved if we believe in Jesus.

NOTES:

_____

_____

_____

_____

_____

_____

_____

_____

IT'S MY LIFE

HOW DO I SAY IT?

IT'S MY LIFE

How Do I Say It?
The Point: Tell My Story
The Passages: Matthew 5:14-16; 10:32-33; 28:19-20; Ephesians 2:1-10

GET STARTED
Lesson 7. How Do I Say It?

GRAPPLE SCHEDULE

5 MINUTES	HANG TIME
10 MINUTES	GRAPPLE CHAT
10-15 MINUTES	GRAPPLE TIME
20-25 MINUTES	TEAM TIME
10 MINUTES	TEAM REPORTS
5 MINUTES	PRAYER & CHALLENGE

SUPPLIES
Bibles, Grapple DVD, DVD player, music CD, CD player, copy of the Grapple Team Guide for each person, paper, pens or pencils, copies of maps printed from a mapping website

BIBLE BASIS FOR TEACHERS
The Passage: Ephesians 2:1-10
In the first chapter of the Apostle Paul's letter to the Ephesians, he asked God to help the believers know God better. He also prayed that they would understand God's power, as well as the hope God gives to those who believe.

In chapter 2, Paul recites where the Ephesians have come from—being spiritually dead, separated totally from God, and (implicitly) unable to revive themselves— and what has happened to them in becoming followers of Jesus. Paul points out in verses 8 and 9 that there's nothing we can do to work our way to salvation, because it is a gift from God. Without what God did for us in his mercy—as undeserving as we are—we would be spiritually dead in our sins with no hope of redemption. And in verse 10, Paul restates that we do good works not to win God's favor but to fulfill what God created us to do. "For we are God's masterpiece," Paul says, and as we do good things, we honor the God who created us and has done so much for us.

How does this relate to the Grapple Question? Often people struggle with the concept of a free gift, especially in the United States. Young adolescents already have it ingrained in their heads that we receive only what we earn. So often kids may be confused when they're told to share a message that completely contradicts what they've come to know as the "truth." It may be a bit of a struggle

to completely comprehend the idea that God would provide us with salvation without asking for anything in exchange. For this lesson, students will grapple with the idea of grace and how they can apply the beautiful message of grace to their own life stories.

How does this connect to Jesus? Jesus is exactly what this question is about. Jesus is the free gift—the turning point of everyone's story. Students will learn how to tell others how they encountered Jesus and accepted his wonderful, free, no-strings-attached gift of salvation. Meeting Jesus changes lives, and this is the part of everyone's personal story that has an impact. Others come to know Jesus when we tell our own stories of how we met and came to love Jesus.

GRAPPLE HANG TIME: 5 MINUTES
Play music as kids enjoy snacks and friendship, and then play an opening countdown from the Grapple DVD to wrap up Grapple Hang Time.

GRAPPLE CHAT: 10 MINUTES
Have students form pairs; if you have an uneven number of kids, it's OK to have one trio in the mix. Ask each group to chat about two of the four topics below that relate to today's grapple topic. (Answers in parentheses are samples.)

IN PAIRS
Chat 1: Find two examples in the Bible of someone telling others about Jesus. (Peter, Acts 4; Stephen, Acts 7; John the Baptist, John 3)

Chat 2: What story have you told to avoid getting in trouble? Did it work?

Chat 3: Find someone in the Bible who was a storyteller. (Jesus, Matthew 13; Nathan, 2 Samuel 12)

Chat 4: What do you appreciate most about your best friend?

GRAPPLE TIME: 10-15 MINUTES
Get Ready: Cue the Grapple DVD to the "It's Your Story" clip.

Lead the entire class in the following:
Let's do an experiment to see how long it takes to get a message to people. The lights in this room are going to go out in 20 seconds (shorten the time if you have a very small class)*, and you need to know what to do when that happens. I'm going to challenge a messenger to see how many people he or she can whisper to—one at a time—in the 20 seconds before the lights go out! Two important instructions: Don't follow the instruction you hear until the lights go out, and if the messenger has whispered the message to you, you may NOT whisper it to anyone else!*

Choose one person to be the messenger. Whisper this message to that person: "When the lights go out, sit cross-legged on the floor." After 20 seconds, briefly turn out the lights. The kids who received the message should be sitting on the floor. Count those kids.

TELL ALL

If you didn't hear the message, how did that feel? How can we spread important messages more quickly?

This time, once you hear the message, you can whisper it to others.

Choose a new message, such as, "When the lights go out, raise both hands in the air."

IN PAIRS

How many more people heard the message this time? What messages or news would you not want your friends to miss out on?

We'll try one more time. As soon as you hear the message, begin doing the action as a way of sharing the message with others.

Choose a new message, such as, "When the lights go out, start clapping your hands."

Why did this method spread the quickest? What factors contributed to the success of this method? How does this activity compare to the importance of hearing and sharing the good news about Jesus?

_____

_____

Let's watch a video to see more about this.

Show the "It's Your Story" clip on the Grapple DVD.

IN PAIRS

How would you feel if you knew your friends had an important message that they chose not to tell you? Is there any reason you wouldn't tell your friends some extremely important news? What are some reasons you don't tell others about Jesus? Explain.

Most Christians know they ought to tell others about their relationship with Jesus. But that's more easily said than done, isn't it? Why can telling our story be so stressful? Why are so many Christians afraid to share their faith? Sometimes people have a hard time finding the right opportunity.

Other times the moment is right, but we just can't find the words. So how do you tell your story? Let's grapple with that!

GRAPPLE TEAM TIME: 20-25 MINUTES
Break into Grapple Teams. Encourage Grapple Team leaders to check in with kids about their week. Grapple Team leaders will facilitate discussion, using the Grapple Team Guide on pages 71-73. Afterward, students will report what they learned.

GRAPPLE TEAM REPORTS: 10 MINUTES
At the end of Grapple Team Time, match Grapple Teams that chose Option 1 with Grapple Teams that chose Option 2 from pages 72-73. Have teams present their reports. (If you have an uneven number of teams, simply form one group of three teams for the presentations. If you have only two Grapple Teams, simply do the presentations one team at a time.)

GRAPPLE PRAYER AND CHALLENGE: 5 MINUTES
Read the Grapple Prayer options. Have the class choose one prayer option that everyone will do. Allow students time to pray about what they discovered. Then close in prayer.

Get Ready: For Option 1, distribute copies of maps printed from a mapping website.

Option 1: Roadmap of Wisdom
Look at a map, and consider all the different roads and highways and streets feature on that map. Pray for God's guidance, wisdom, and direction in your life, and ask God for strength in following the path and plan he has created for you.

Option 2: Lectio Divina
Get comfortable, preferably sitting apart from each other. Read a Bible passage aloud, and then remain in silence for a few minutes and think about the verses. Close your eyes and breathe deeply. Then read aloud Romans 8:35-39, slowly and with feeling. Then read it two more times the same way. Finally, allow a few minutes to silently bask in God's love.

GRAPPLE CHALLENGE
The thought of sharing the gospel with someone can be overwhelming. What if you forget important parts? Or what if the person doesn't believe in the Bible and starts arguing with you?

No one can argue with you about your own testimony, so that's a great place to start when sharing your faith. By focusing on how the gospel has affected you personally, you show someone the most important part of being a Christian: your relationship with Jesus. This week, take that relationship public. Commit to telling one friend, relative, or stranger about your awesome friend. Then do it!

WEEKLY GRAPPLE CONNECTION
(You can use this as an email template to send to parents)

Grapple Question: How Do I Say It?
Kids Learn: Tell My Story
Dig Into the Bible: Ephesians 2:1-10

Most Christians know they ought to tell others about their relationship with Jesus. But that's more easily said than done—no matter your age. Why can telling your story be so stressful? Why are so many Christians afraid to share their faith? Sometimes people have a hard time finding the right opportunity. But other times, when the moment is right, we just can't find the words.

No one can argue with you over your own testimony. This is always a great place to start when sharing your faith. By focusing on how the gospel has impacted you personally, you focus on the most important part of being a Christian: your relationship with Jesus. Practice telling your testimony with your child. Sharing your story is a good way to start sharing your faith!

- -

LESSON 7

In your Grapple Team, use this guide to grapple with today's question.

Sharing your faith with others can be fun; it also can be really intimidating sometimes.

IN PAIRS

What are three excuses people might give for not sharing their faith with others? What is the biggest thing that holds you back? Have you ever had a good experience when you talked about Jesus? Describe it.

Close your eyes, and think about a time you were nervous or scared about being in the dark. Maybe the electricity went out during a storm, or maybe someone suddenly turned off the lights in a room. What did you think? How did you feel when the lights came on again?

People who don't know Jesus are living in spiritual darkness.

Read Matthew 5:14-16.

How can we bring spiritual light to those who live in darkness because they don't know about Jesus? What do we do when people don't want the light to shine on their darkness?

_____

_____

Read Matthew 10:32-33 and Matthew 28:19-20.

IN PAIRS

According to these passages, what motivates us to share our faith? What situations have you been in where you didn't feel comfortable sharing your faith? What fears stop you from sharing your story with others? How do you feel when you're left out of something really great? How can thinking about those feelings of exclusion help you include others in the good news of Jesus?

Read Ephesians 2:1-10.

Write down key phrases from this passage that remind you of the importance of having a relationship with Jesus.

_____

_____

IN PAIRS

God offered us an amazing, free gift by sending Jesus. In what ways do we typically respond when we receive gifts? Share how you feel about your relationship with Jesus, and then brainstorm a natural response to those feelings.

Let's be prepared! Every Christian has a unique story of how they came to know Jesus as their friend. Sharing your story is a good way to start sharing your faith! On a separate sheet of paper, answer these questions:

S—Before you knew Jesus, what made God sad about your life?
H—How did you hear about Jesus?
A—When did you ask Jesus to be your friend and Savior?
R—How has your relationship with Jesus changed your life?
E—What makes you excited about God?

GRAPPLE TEAM REPORTS

With your team, choose one of the options below to report what you discovered.

Option 1: Relay Report

Discuss some of the big ideas you've learned today. Once you're ready to make your presentation to the other team, line up on one side of the room. Run down to the other end of the room and back. When you return, tell about something you learned today. Then the next person in line runs to the end of the room and back, and reports something else. Continue until everyone has participated.

Option 2: Proverb It

Look through the book of Proverbs and find one verse that best connects to what you learned today. If you have enough time, consider finding additional verses.

HOW DO I SAY IT?

Acts 1:8

"But you will receive power when the Holy Spirit comes upon you. And you will be my witnesses, telling people about me everywhere—in Jerusalem, throughout Judea, in Samaria, and to the ends of the earth."

GRAPPLE CHAT

Chat 1: Find two examples in the Bible of someone telling others about Jesus.

Chat 2: What story have you told to avoid getting in trouble? Did it work?

Chat 3: Find someone in the Bible who was a storyteller.

Chat 4: What do you appreciate most about your best friend?

GRAPPLE CHALLENGE

Tell your story to someone this week. Tell that person how your relationship with Jesus has transformed your life.

NOTES:

_____

_____

_____

_____

_____

_____

_____

_____

_____

_____

IT'S MY LIFE

CAN I SAY IT WRONG?

IT'S MY LIFE

Can I Say It Wrong?
The Point: Know My Audience
The Passage: Acts 17:16-34

GET STARTED
Lesson 8. Can I Say It Wrong?

GRAPPLE SCHEDULE

5 MINUTES	HANG TIME
10 MINUTES	GRAPPLE CHAT
10-15 MINUTES	GRAPPLE TIME
20-25 MINUTES	TEAM TIME
10 MINUTES	TEAM REPORTS
5 MINUTES	PRAYER & CHALLENGE

SUPPLIES
Bibles, Grapple DVD, DVD player, music CD, CD player, copy of the Grapple Team Guide for each person, paper, pens or pencils

BIBLE BASIS FOR TEACHERS
The Passage: Acts 17:16-34
In this passage, Paul was waiting for Silas and Timothy to join him in Athens, and he was troubled by the false idols he saw there. So Paul engaged with the religious people and the philosophers and discussed the truth of God with them.

Paul's audience included adherents of the Epicurean and Stoic philosophies. Both philosophies held that humanity's ultimate purpose is to achieve wisdom and knowledge. The Epicureans believed that any gods that existed were unconcerned with human beings; therefore, they pursued knowledge by maximizing pleasure and avoiding pain. The Stoics didn't strongly differentiate god from nature or knowledge, and they believed that one could achieve wisdom by controlling one's passions, enduring pain, and avoiding pleasure.

Paul addressed these Athenians by commending them for their religiousness but then pointing out an altar they had built "to an Unknown God." Paul declared that their Unknown God was, in fact, the one true God. He testified that the true God "made the world and everything in it" and is intimately involved in human activities. Paul told them that true wisdom, pleasure, and joy come only from God.

Paul continued to relate God's truth to what the people knew. In verse 28, he even quoted from two ancient poets of the region: Epimenides and Aratus. Paul quoted these poets in an effort to connect the true story of God with the stories the people already knew about their false gods. Paul was totally convinced that the God he served was the only true God, the creator of heaven and earth, the all-powerful one who needed nothing from humans but reached out and gave us what we needed: salvation through the death and resurrection of God's Son, Jesus Christ!

How does this relate to the Grapple Question? There is an individual, special, and specific way each person tells a story. There's also an individual, special, and specific way each person prefers to hear a story. When kids set out to have an impact on the world by sharing Jesus with others, it is important that they know their own style for sharing as well as the preferred style of the audience. Students may wonder what style works best for them. Paul had to figure out a way to reach out to the Athenians specifically—and he did. In the same way, kids should become aware of the different ways they can approach others in order to maximize their efforts.

How does this connect to Jesus? Jesus didn't stick to one methodology either. Jesus preached in the synagogues and the Temple to the religious leaders; he told parables to the common farmers and laborers; and he healed the sick, the paralyzed, and the blind. Jesus found the best ways to connect with people. He wants us to do the same.

GRAPPLE HANG TIME: 5 MINUTES
Play music as kids enjoy snacks and friendship, and then play an opening countdown from the Grapple DVD to wrap up Grapple Hang Time.

GRAPPLE CHAT: 10 MINUTES
Have students form pairs; if you have an uneven number of kids, it's OK to have one trio in the mix. Ask each group to chat about two of the four topics below that relate to today's grapple topic. (Answers in parentheses are samples.)

IN PAIRS
Chat 1: Find two men in the Bible who claimed to have trouble speaking. (Moses, Exodus 4:10; Paul, 2 Corinthians 11:6)

Chat 2: Think about the longest phone conversation you've ever had. Who were you talking with, and how long did your call last?

Chat 3: Discover who Solomon's audience was and why people wanted to hear him. (People from every nation came to hear God's wisdom, 1 Kings 10:24; kings from every nation came to hear God's wisdom, 2 Chronicles 9:23)

Chat 4: When have you performed for an audience? What did you do, and how did the experience make you feel?

GRAPPLE TIME: 10-15 MINUTES
Get Ready: Cue the Grapple DVD to the "Say Something" clip.

Lead the entire class in the following:
How did you celebrate your most recent birthday? That's the topic for the next few minutes as you mill around talking and listening to each other. However, you can only use words that start with the first letter of your first name. Got it? Go!

After a minute, allow kids to use the first letters of their middle and last names as well. After another minute allow kids to use words that start with any letter that appears in their first, middle, and last names.

TELL ALL
How well were you able to communicate? How well were you able to understand what other people were saying? How did the experience change as you had more letters to work with?

IN PAIRS
How do you feel about speaking in front of groups? Are there any topics that leave you feeling tongue-tied, and if so, which topics?

Show the "Say Something" clip on the Grapple DVD.

Some of us are better speakers than others, but we can all use practice communicating. Even the best communicators sometimes say things wrong. Or they may say it clearly, but their listeners misunderstand. Let's grapple with the question of whether we might say it wrong.

GRAPPLE TEAM TIME: 20-25 MINUTES
Break into Grapple Teams. Encourage Grapple Team leaders to check in with kids about their week. Grapple Team leaders will facilitate discussion, using the Grapple Team Guide on pages 83-85. Afterward, students will report what they learned.

GRAPPLE TEAM REPORTS: 10 MINUTES
At the end of Grapple Team Time, match Grapple Teams that chose Option 1 with Grapple Teams that chose Option 2 from page 85. Have teams present their reports. (If you have an uneven number of teams, simply form one group of three teams for the presentations. If you have only two Grapple Teams, simply do the presentations one team at a time.)

GRAPPLE PRAYER AND CHALLENGE: 5 MINUTES

Read the Grapple Prayer options. Have the class choose one prayer option that everyone will do. Allow students time to pray about what they discovered. Then close in prayer.

Get Ready: For Option 1, distribute paper and make sure students have pens or pencils.

Option 1: Letter Prayers

Write a letter to Jesus. Tell him what you know is true about him and what you're unsure about; ask for his strength and help in developing a deeper trust in him.

Option 2: Strong Foundation

Stand up, and close your eyes. While balancing on one foot, silently ask God to help you with a challenging situation you're facing right now. Stay in this position as long as you can—up to two minutes, if possible. Then stand on two feet and ask God to help you be a person who will stand confidently in God's strength.

GRAPPLE CHALLENGE

Can you say it wrong? Yes. You can say it badly. But even if you say it clearly, others may not understand what you have to say. People called the Apostle Paul a babbler of strange ideas. Ultimately, you aren't responsible for the end result. God asks you to be his witness; the results are between God and the person to whom you witness. In Matthew 10:18-20, Jesus assured his followers that the Holy Spirit would be with them and give them the right words to say when they spoke as his witnesses. This week I challenge you: Trust the Spirit to give you the opportunity and the words that are appropriate to the style God has given you and to the person to whom you're speaking, and trust God to work his results in people's lives. Take the risk, and trust God!

WEEKLY GRAPPLE CONNECTION
(You can use this as an email template to send to parents)

Grapple Question: Can I Say It Wrong?
Kids Learn: Know My Audience
Dig Into the Bible: Acts 17:16-34

When it comes to talking about Jesus, Christians often are afraid that they won't say the right thing. Some of us are better speakers than others, but even the best communicators sometimes say things wrong—or they may say it right, but their listeners misunderstand.

Sometimes we worry that we may say it wrong or that others may not always understand what we have to say. But we can relax—the end result is not up to us. In Matthew 10:18-20, Jesus assured his followers that the Holy Spirit would be with them and give them the right words to say when they spoke as his witnesses. With your child, practice what you could say to share your faith—it's always good to be prepared. Then jump in and do it! Tell one person this week about having a relationship with Jesus, and encourage your child to do the same. Regardless of how you think it will go, remember that God can use any situation for his glory.

- -

LESSON 8

In your Grapple Team, use this guide to grapple with today's question.

Share with your team a story—if you have one—about something embarrassing that happened to you. If the story involves public speaking, all the better!

What do you think makes an embarrassing moment embarrassing? For example, if you said or did the same thing in front of two different individuals or groups, would it be embarrassing both times?

IN PAIRS

On a scale of one to five, how easily do you get embarrassed? On a scale of one to five, how willing are you to risk embarrassment in order to share Jesus with others?

Let's take a close look at how the Apostle Paul shared with people about Jesus.

Read Acts 17:16-34.

Where and to whom did Paul talk about Jesus? What places or people in your life might provide opportunities to share the good news of Jesus?

Paul	Me
_____	_____
_____	_____
_____	_____
_____	_____

What do you notice about what Paul says? What can you learn from Paul's example?

Paul	Me
_____	_____
_____	_____
_____	_____
_____	_____

How do you think talking about something from their own culture made the people feel? Why do you think people responded to Paul and his message the way they did? What does that tell you about evangelism?

_____

_____

Paul noticed something about the Athenian people and used that as a starting place to talk with them about Jesus. But Paul also knew his own style. Read the following descriptions of evangelism styles. Circle the one that you think best describes your own style. Put a triangle around the one you think describes Paul's style.

- Confrontational: Ask direct questions and expect direct responses.
- Intellectual: Use logical arguments to defend a position.
- Testimonial: Let your own story do all the talking.
- Interpersonal: Use your personal relationship to share on an intimate level.
- Invitational: Invite someone to church or other Christ-centered events.
- Service: Do good things for people in Christ's name.

IN PAIRS
Which of the evangelism styles did you circle, and why? When have you had an opportunity to use any of these styles? When you're sharing the gospel with someone, do you think it's more important to use your style or their style, and why? With whom can you share Jesus with this week? How do you think you'll go about it?

GRAPPLE TEAM REPORTS

With your team, choose one of the options below to report what you discovered.

Option 1: Instant Object Lesson

Use whatever you can find around you to create some instant object lessons that explain what you learned today. Get creative!

Option 2: Movie Illustration

Together, think of a scene from a movie that illustrates what you learned today. Be prepared to describe that scene and explain why it illustrates what you've learned.

CAN I SAY IT WRONG?

Acts 1:8
"But you will receive power when the Holy Spirit comes upon you. And you will be my witnesses, telling people about me everywhere—in Jerusalem, throughout Judea, in Samaria, and to the ends of the earth."

GRAPPLE CHAT
Chat 1: Find two men in the Bible who claimed to have trouble speaking.

Chat 2: Think about the longest phone conversation you've ever had. Who were you talking with, and how long did your call last?

Chat 3: Discover who Solomon's audience was and why people wanted to hear him.

Chat 4: When have you performed for an audience? What did you do, and how did the experience make you feel?

GRAPPLE CHALLENGE
This week ask the Holy Spirit to give you the right words and the right ways to speak to others about Jesus.

NOTES:

_____

_____

_____

_____

_____

_____

_____

_____

_____

CROSSES, CRESCENTS, AND CAPRICORNS

WHY ARE THERE SO MANY?

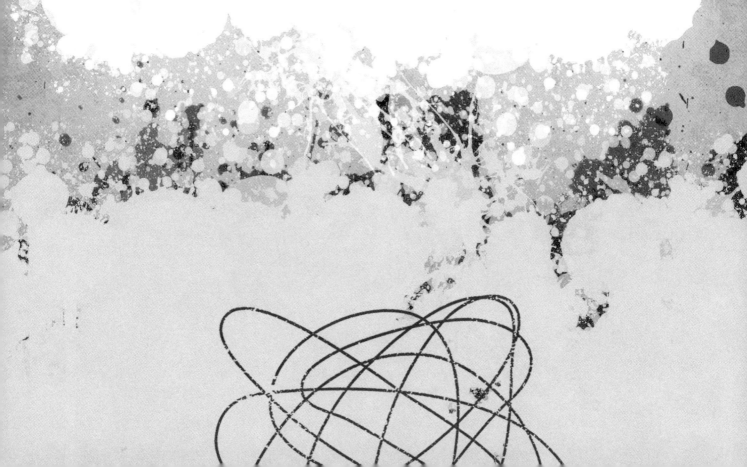

CROSSES, CRESCENTS, AND CAPRICORNS

Why Are There So Many?
The Point: We Are the Body of Christ
The Passages: Acts 10:34-48; 1 Corinthians 12:12-26; Ephesians 4:1-16;
Philippians 2:1-11

GET STARTED
Lesson 9. Why Are There So Many?

GRAPPLE SCHEDULE

5 MINUTES	HANG TIME
10 MINUTES	GRAPPLE CHAT
10-15 MINUTES	GRAPPLE TIME
20-25 MINUTES	TEAM TIME
10 MINUTES	TEAM REPORTS
5 MINUTES	PRAYER & CHALLENGE

SUPPLIES
Bibles, Grapple DVD, DVD player, music CD, CD player, copy of the Grapple Team Guide for each person, paper, pens or pencils

BIBLE BASIS FOR TEACHERS
The Passage: 1 Corinthians 12:12-26
In this passage, Paul introduces to the Corinthians the concept that the church is like a body—more specifically, the body of Christ. From 1 Corinthians 12:1, we can infer that the Corinthians had raised questions about spiritual gifts, and from some of Paul's comments in the passage, we might infer that they disagreed over whose spiritual gifts were most important. Apparently some people were feeling insignificant because of their gifts (1 Corinthians 12:14-20), and others were feeling overly important because of their gifts (1 Corinthians 12:21-26).

Paul's message is a great equalizer: People with gifts that seem insignificant are actually much more important than they may think, and people with gifts that seem more spectacular aren't any more important than anyone else. An important truth to note can be found in verse 18: "Our bodies have many parts, and God has put each part just where he wants it."

In a body, if one part is hurting, the other parts feel the hurt. And if one part feels great, it makes all of the body feel better! That's how the church should be! God gives different gifts for building up the body of Christ. We all are part of that body, and God wants us to use the gifts we've received to fill the place intended for us in the church.

That's how we'll be most fulfilled and how we'll work together with other Christians to further God's kingdom on earth.

How does this relate to the Grapple Question? In this lesson, students will grapple with why so many Christian denominations exist. This lesson will help guide kids into understanding the foundational attributes of Christianity (the major doctrinal topics). This lesson also will help kids grapple with the debated minors (things that end up dividing people within the church, resulting in different denominations). While 1 Corinthians 12 specifically addresses divisions over spiritual gifts, the principle remains relevant and applicable: We are one body with many parts, and we can all work together to build up the body of Christ as we continue to live out God's commission on earth.

How does this connect to Jesus? The church is one body, and that's how Jesus set it up—one body with many parts. Denominations spring up because of the many different parts. Help students grapple with whether denominations actually divide the body or contribute to its success in mission and ministry.

GRAPPLE HANG TIME: 5 MINUTES
Play music as kids enjoy snacks and friendship, and then play an opening countdown from the Grapple DVD to wrap up Grapple Hang Time.

GRAPPLE CHAT: 10 MINUTES
Have students form pairs; if you have an uneven number of kids, it's OK to have one trio in the mix. Ask each group to chat about two of the four topics below that relate to today's grapple topic. (Answers in parentheses are samples.)

IN PAIRS
Chat 1: Name two people in the Bible who worked together to accomplish something. (Esther and Mordecai, Esther 2–8)

Chat 2: What is your favorite group activity—such as sports, board games, or school projects—and why?

Chat 3: Name one thing that divided the early church. (Including Gentiles, Acts 11)

Chat 4: Excluding your birthdates or your favorite food, what are three things you and your partner don't have in common?

GRAPPLE TIME: 10-15 MINUTES
Get Ready: Cue the Grapple DVD to the "The Tree" clip.

Lead the entire class in the following:

Give each person a blank sheet of paper and pen or pencil.

Let's find out how much we all have in common. As I read each question, write your answer on your paper.
- *What is your favorite color?*
- *What is the last movie you saw?*
- *What time do you wake up for school?*
- *What is your favorite thing to do in your free time?*
- *How many people are in your family, including you?*
- *Other than Jesus, who is your favorite person in the Bible?*
- *If you had to stake your life on one belief, what would it be?*

Now compare your answers to others' in the class. Is there anyone who had seven answers that matched yours exactly?

Allow a few moments for kids to compare answers.

TELL ALL
Did anyone have exactly the same answers for all the questions? Tell us about the person you had the most in common with. How many of your answers matched? Why would God make us all so different?

IN PAIRS
We all have differences, but is it OK for Christians to have big differences in our beliefs about sin, baptism, or Jesus' death? Why or why not? What aspects of Christianity should we all agree on? What aspects are OK to disagree about, if any?

Let's watch a DVD to learn more about this.

Show "The Tree" on the Grapple DVD.

Have you ever noticed how many different denominations there are? We all call ourselves Christians, so what's the difference? Are there any similarities? Why are there so many different beliefs about Jesus? Let's grapple with that.

GRAPPLE TEAM TIME: 20-25 MINUTES
Break into Grapple Teams. Encourage Grapple Team leaders to check in with kids about their week. Grapple Team leaders will facilitate discussion, using the Grapple Team Guide on pages 95-96. Afterward, students will report what they learned.

GRAPPLE TEAM REPORTS: 10 MINUTES

At the end of Grapple Team Time, match Grapple Teams that chose Option 1 with Grapple Teams that chose Option 2 from page 96. Have teams present their reports. (If you have an uneven number of teams, simply form one group of three teams for the presentations. If you have only two Grapple Teams, simply do the presentations one team at a time.)

GRAPPLE PRAYER AND CHALLENGE: 5 MINUTES

Read the Grapple Prayer options. Have the class choose one prayer option that everyone will do. Allow students time to pray about what they discovered. Then close in prayer.

Get Ready: For Option 2, make sure students have paper and pens or pencils.

Option 1: Prayer Partners

Find a partner to pray with. Talk about troubles you currently face, especially anything connected to today's lesson. Then pray for each other to be able to see your situation from God's perspective.

Option 2: Prayer Pile

Get in a circle with the rest of your group. Write a prayer to God. Then crumple up the paper with the prayer on it and make a pile of crumpled papers in the middle of the circle. Choose one crumpled prayer from the pile. Silently pray the words written on the paper, and then ask God to answer the prayer for the person who wrote it.

GRAPPLE CHALLENGE

Different denominations believe different things about certain subjects, including baptism, the End Times, and women in positions of leadership. But there are some things that the Bible clearly states. Jesus was perfect and didn't sin. God, Jesus, and the Holy Spirit form the Trinity. Jesus died for our sins. We can have everlasting life through our relationship with Jesus.

This week, tell one person about your absolute belief in those areas. You could tell someone who attends a church of a different denomination or someone who has never even heard the message of Jesus before. Be willing to discuss and debate other things, but stand strong for the absolutes.

WEEKLY GRAPPLE CONNECTION
(You can use this as an email template to send to parents)

Grapple Question: Why Are There So Many?
Kids Learn: We Are the Body of Christ
Dig Into the Bible: 1 Corinthians 12:12-26

Have you ever noticed how many different Christian denominations there are? Different denominations believe different things about certain subjects, like baptism, the End Times, and women in positions of leadership.

Do this with your child: Look in your local phonebook under "churches"—or use an online search engine—and observe the many different types. Pick one denomination that catches your attention (maybe you have a friend that attends a church of that denomination). Then do some online research to find what is similar to and different from your own denomination. (Try religionfacts.com, or just type the name of the denomination and "beliefs" into a search engine.)

There are some things that the Bible clearly outlines: Jesus was perfect and didn't sin; God, Jesus, and the Holy Spirit form the Trinity; Jesus died for our sins; we can have everlasting life through our relationship with Jesus. Talk to your child about how it's good to be willing to discuss and debate other topics, but it's also important to stand strong for the absolutes.

- -

LESSON 9
In your Grapple Team, use this guide to grapple with today's question.

Do different denominations divide the church body, or can they actually help bring more people to Christ? Let's look into that.

Read Acts 10:34-48.

IN PAIRS
According to this passage, what two things are necessary to gain God's acceptance? What are some other things that you've seen denominations, or even individual people who are Christians, disagree about?

Read 1 Corinthians 12:12-26.

Paul assured the church of Corinth that one person's gifts aren't any more important than another's. In fact, we can all use our gifts to contribute to the church body as a whole. When have you seen the body of Christ working together to accomplish something big?

When have you felt like your gifts and abilities mattered in accomplishing something, and why?

_____

_____

IN PAIRS

In our human bodies, all of the parts have to work together to function. How does that apply to the church body? If the different "body parts" refer to different denominations, what are some obstacles we'd have to overcome to work more closely together?

Read Philippians 2:1-11 and Ephesians 4:1-16.

List three things you learned from these passages about how God expects us to relate to other Christians, even if our beliefs about some things are different.

_____

_____

_____

GRAPPLE TEAM REPORTS

With your team, choose one of the options below to report what you discovered.

Option 1: Project Youth!

With your team, choose your three best ideas about how you could help the youth group learn about today's lesson and put its truths into practice. Be prepared to explain why these truths are important for teenagers to believe and follow.

Option 2: Preach It; Practice It

Create a short instruction manual titled "Practice What You Preach." Come up with at least 10 ways everyone can put today's lesson into practice this next week.

WHY ARE THERE SO MANY?

1 Peter 3:15
Instead, you must worship Christ as Lord of your life. And if someone asks about your Christian hope, always be ready to explain it.

GRAPPLE CHAT

Chat 1: Name two people in the Bible who worked together to accomplish something.

Chat 2: What is your favorite group activity—such as sports, board games, or school projects—and why?

Chat 3: Name one thing that divided the early church.

Chat 4: Excluding your birthdates or your favorite food, what are three things you and your partner don't have in common?

GRAPPLE CHALLENGE

This week, have a discussion about beliefs with one person from a Christian denomination different from yours.

NOTES:

_____

_____

_____

_____

_____

_____

_____

_____

_____

_____

CROSSES, CRESCENTS, AND CAPRICORNS

ARE THEY CHRISTIANS?

CROSSES, CRESCENTS, AND CAPRICORNS

Are They Christians?
The Point: The Trinity Is Important to My Faith
The Passages: John 14:9-10, 16-18; Acts 2:22-41

GET STARTED
Lesson 10. The Trinity Is Important to My Faith

GRAPPLE SCHEDULE

5 MINUTES	HANG TIME
10 MINUTES	GRAPPLE CHAT
10-15 MINUTES	GRAPPLE TIME
20-25 MINUTES	TEAM TIME
10 MINUTES	TEAM REPORTS
5 MINUTES	PRAYER & CHALLENGE

SUPPLIES
Bibles, Grapple DVD, DVD player, music CD, CD player, copy of the Grapple Team Guide for each person, paper, pens or pencils, modeling dough

BIBLE BASIS FOR TEACHERS
The Passage: Acts 2:22-41
These Christians were meeting together during the Jewish celebration of Pentecost that celebrated the harvest and commemorated the giving of the Law of Moses. While gathered together, they heard the roar of a strong wind. A small flame rested above each person in the room. Through the power of the Holy Spirit, the Christians began speaking about Jesus in other languages.

Some of the people who witnessed this event were amazed. Others assumed the Christians were drunk. Peter stepped forward and helped the crowd understand that the Holy Spirit had filled them just like God promised in Scripture (see Joel 2:28-29). In a powerful sermon, Peter explained who Jesus was and how David prophesied about him hundreds of years before. Peter explained that God the Father raised Jesus from the dead and exalted him to the highest honor in heaven. Furthermore, the Holy Spirit is to be poured out upon all of Jesus' followers.

How does this relate to the Grapple Question? Jesus had promised to send the Holy Spirit to his followers, and the Holy Spirit came in a dramatic, unmistakable fashion. It's significant that the Holy Spirit came during the celebration of Pentecost. Many Jews made a pilgrimage to the Holy Land for the celebration commemorating the day God gave the Law to Moses.

For Christians, it became the day God first gave his Holy Spirit to those who believe in Jesus. On the day of Pentecost—upon the birth of the church—the Trinity was embraced and taught. The Bible tells us that 3,000 people decided to follow Jesus, were baptized, and joined the church that very day.

How does this connect to Jesus? Without the help and power of the Holy Spirit, we can't do anything with eternal value and significance. The Holy Spirit gave the early Christians the ability to reach the people around them. They were able to share the message of Jesus with people from other cultures. Peter was able to give a message that cut to people's hearts so dramatically that thousands became Christians in one day. Upon the day of Pentecost, all three persons of the Trinity were embraced.

GRAPPLE HANG TIME: 5 MINUTES
Play music as kids enjoy snacks and friendship, and then play an opening countdown from the Grapple DVD to wrap up Grapple Hang Time.

GRAPPLE CHAT: 10 MINUTES
Have students form pairs; if you have an uneven number of kids, it's OK to have one trio in the mix. Ask each group to chat about two of the four topics below that relate to today's grapple topic. (Answers in parentheses are samples.)

IN PAIRS
Chat 1: Find some different ways the Holy Spirit is symbolized in the Bible. (A dove, Matthew 3:16; wind, Acts 2:2; fire, Acts 2:3)

Chat 2: Which three flavors of ice cream would you like to blend together into one brand-new product, and why?

Chat 3: Discover what the following Bible verses have in common: Mark 12:32; Romans 3:30; 1 Corinthians 8:6; and 1 Timothy 2:5. (They all state that there is only one God)

Chat 4: Do you know any family with triplets? What do you think it would be like to have triplets in your family—or to be a triplet?

GRAPPLE TIME: 10-15 MINUTES
Get Ready: Cue the Grapple DVD to the "One, Two, Three" clip.

Lead the entire class in the following:

Have kids get into their Grapple Teams. Give each team some modeling dough.

This game is called What's Inside? Each team will have three minutes to find small objects throughout the room or things you may already have, such as candy, erasers, or coins.

Wrap each object with modeling dough so it's completely hidden, and then return to your seats with the wrapped objects.

Instruct kids to begin their search, and let them know when three minutes is up.

Pair off with someone on another team, and exchange wrapped objects. Ask each other up to five yes-or-no questions about the hidden object to figure out what it is.

TELL ALL
How would you have figured out what objects were hidden inside if you couldn't ask questions—or would you have figured it out? Looking back, what are some better questions you might have asked?

IN PAIRS
When they were covered with modeling dough, all the objects looked basically the same. Often different religious groups also look, act, and talk the same. What are some good questions we can ask to determine which groups are truly Christian? What are some basic truths of Christianity that make it different from other religions?

Show the "One, Two, Three" clip on the Grapple DVD.

Sometimes it's hard to tell different religious groups apart. Most are often made up of good people who act lovingly and help others. But at the same time, some worship many gods, and others say that Jesus was just another good person but wasn't God. So are these people Christian? How can you tell who's Christian and who isn't? Why should it matter to you to find out? After all, aren't we supposed to be accepting of all people? Let's grapple with that!

GRAPPLE TEAM TIME: 20-25 MINUTES
Break into Grapple Teams. Encourage Grapple Team leaders to check in with kids about their week. Grapple Team leaders will facilitate discussion, using the Grapple Team Guide on pages 105-106. Afterward, students will report what they learned.

GRAPPLE TEAM REPORTS: 10 MINUTES
At the end of Grapple Team Time, match Grapple Teams that chose Option 1 with Grapple Teams that chose Option 2 from page 106. Have teams present their reports. (If you have an uneven number of teams, simply form one group of three teams for the presentations. If you have only two Grapple Teams, simply do the presentations one team at a time.)

GRAPPLE PRAYER AND CHALLENGE: 5 MINUTES

Read the Grapple Prayer options. Have the class choose one prayer option that everyone will do. Allow students time to pray about what they discovered. Then close in prayer.

Option 1: You Are; I Am

Find a partner to pray with. God gave us the Bible so we could know him and so we could know who we really are. Take turns each praying a one-sentence prayer that starts, "God, you are…." Then take turns each praying a one-sentence prayer that starts with the words: "Because of your love for me, God, I am…."

Option 2: Word Prayers

Take a quiet moment to consider what you know about God. Then prayerfully call out one or two words that describe who God is, such as *Comforter, Protector, Provider,* or *Shepherd.*

GRAPPLE CHALLENGE

Most people will tell you they believe in God, but that doesn't mean they're Christians. Christianity teaches that God the Father; his Son, Jesus; and the Holy Spirit are all one—and the only—God. When people tell you they believe in God, ask if they also believe in the Trinity and in only one God. The answer might surprise you!

WEEKLY GRAPPLE CONNECTION
(You can use this as an email template to send to parents)

Grapple Question: Are They Christians?
Kids Learn: The Trinity Is Important to My Faith
Dig Into the Bible: Acts 2:22-41

Sometimes it's hard to tell different religious groups apart. Most are often made up of good people who act lovingly and help others. But at the same time, some worship many gods, and others say that Jesus was just another good person.

Ask your child about his or her friends. Are they Christians? Many people will tell you they believe in God, but that doesn't mean they're Christians. Christianity teaches that God the Father; his Son, Jesus; and the Holy Spirit are all one—and the only—God. Do your child's friends measure up to this standard? Discuss how to be friends with someone who doesn't share your core beliefs, and the importance of being built up by some friends who do. Share an example from your own life about standing strong for your faith.

LESSON 10

In your Grapple Team, use this guide to grapple with today's question.

Our world is made up of many different religious groups that have their own beliefs about who God is. List on a piece of paper at least five religious groups, along with one or two things you know about what each one believes.

IN PAIRS

Share your answers. Make a chart together on another sheet of paper. List each religious group down the left side of your paper with columns across the top labeled "One God?" "Many Gods?" and "Who Is Jesus?" Complete the chart, answering the questions for each group.

Read aloud John 14:9-10.

Jesus says anyone who saw him also saw the Father because he's in the Father and the Father is in him. Draw or describe something—either natural or man-made—that illustrates Jesus' relationship with God the Father. How is this view of Jesus different from other religions' understanding of Jesus?

_____

_____

Read aloud John 14:16-18.

Jesus told his disciples that after he went to heaven, his Father would send the Holy Spirit to be with them forever. Even though Jesus was leaving the earth, in verse 18 he promised, "I will not abandon you as orphans—I will come to you." How are we able to know Jesus, even though we can't see him or (usually) hear him or touch him? What does Jesus' promise of the Holy Spirit mean for you today?

_____

_____

Read Acts 2:22-41.

IN PAIRS

Based on what Peter said, write single words or phrases to describe the relationship among God the Father, Jesus, and the Holy Spirit. Then take turns explaining to each other how you believe God can be three persons yet only one God, and why this truth is important to the gospel message.

_____

_____

Why is it important to know what other religious groups believe?

_____

_____

If Jesus is not God and the Holy Spirit was not given to us when Jesus went to heaven, then there cannot be a gospel message of salvation, and Christianity cannot be true. How do these truths help you in wanting to reach out to other religious groups?

What has changed, if anything, in your views of other religious groups now that you know how they differ from Christianity?

_____

_____

GRAPPLE TEAM REPORTS

With your team, choose one of the options below to report what you discovered.

Get Ready: For Option 1, distribute modeling dough—or have students "recycle" the modeling dough from the earlier activity.

Option 1: Sculpt It
Take some modeling dough, and sculpt objects that explain or reveal what you discovered today. Be prepared to interpret your artwork in case you tend to create abstract art!

Option 2: Dialogue
Create a scene from your everyday life that includes dialogue involving everyone on your team (or several sample conversations) to demonstrate what you've learned today.

ARE THEY CHRISTIANS?

1 Peter 3:15
Instead, you must worship Christ as Lord of your life. And if someone asks about your Christian hope, always be ready to explain it.

GRAPPLE CHAT
Chat 1: Find some different ways the Holy Spirit is symbolized in the Bible.

Chat 2: Which three flavors of ice cream would you like to blend together into one brand-new product, and why?

Chat 3: Discover what the following Bible verses have in common: Mark 12:32; Romans 3:30; 1 Corinthians 8:6; and 1 Timothy 2:5.

Chat 4: Do you know any family with triplets? What do you think it would be like to have triplets in your family—or to be a triplet?

GRAPPLE CHALLENGE
This week, when people tell you they believe in God, ask if they also believe in the Trinity and in only one God.

NOTES:

_____

_____

_____

_____

_____

_____

_____

_____

_____

_____

CROSSES, CRESCENTS, AND CAPRICORNS

IS IT EVIL?

CROSSES, CRESCENTS, AND CAPRICORNS

Is It Evil?
The Point: The Spiritual World Is Real—So I Will Seek God Only
The Passages: Deuteronomy 4:25; 18:9-14; Amos 5:14-15; Matthew 15:18-20; Mark 1:23-28; Luke 4:1-13; John 17:13-21; Galatians 5:17-21; Ephesians 6:10-18; James 1:14-16

GET STARTED
Lesson 11. Is It Evil?

GRAPPLE SCHEDULE

5 MINUTES	HANG TIME
10 MINUTES	GRAPPLE CHAT
10-15 MINUTES	GRAPPLE TIME
20-25 MINUTES	TEAM TIME
10 MINUTES	TEAM REPORTS
5 MINUTES	PRAYER & CHALLENGE

SUPPLIES
Bibles, Grapple DVD, DVD player, music CD, CD player, copy of the Grapple Team Guide for each person, paper, pens or pencils, newsprint or butcher paper, markers, masking tape

BIBLE BASIS FOR TEACHERS
The Passage: Deuteronomy 18:9-22
As the people of Israel entered the land of Canaan, they began to encounter the local Canaanites and discovered that these people employed other means when trying to communicate with their pagan gods. Some of these forms of communication had the potential to tempt the Israelites to emulate them. God found these practices detestable in every way and instructed the Israelites to drive the Canaanites out of the land. God forbade not only the worship of false gods but also the ways the Canaanites attempted to communicate with these false gods. The Israelites were told to shun such practices as human sacrifice, fortunetelling, sorcery, interpreting omens, witchcraft, casting spells, functioning as a medium or psychic, and consulting the dead.

How does this relate to the Grapple Question? This lesson will help kids grapple with something many adolescents are curious about: the occult. Students will look at Deuteronomy 18 and see what God has to say about the occult. They'll discuss the risks of such things as Ouija boards, mediums, and fortunetellers. They'll examine questions about the validity of the spiritual world and at what level, if at all, they should interact with that world.

How does this connect to Jesus? Jesus addressed the spiritual world when he cast out demons and fought off the temptations of the devil. This lesson will help students understand that God will provide us with everything we need and that seeking answers from the occult is dangerous.

GRAPPLE HANG TIME: 5 MINUTES
Play music as kids enjoy snacks and friendship, and then play an opening countdown from the Grapple DVD to wrap up Grapple Hang Time.

GRAPPLE CHAT: 10 MINUTES
Have students form pairs; if you have an uneven number of kids, it's OK to have one trio in the mix. Ask each group to chat about two of the four topics below that relate to today's grapple topic. (Answers in parentheses are samples.)

IN PAIRS
Chat 1: Find at least one Bible "villain" and what he or she did that was bad. (Cain, the first murderer, Genesis 4; Judas, the disciple who betrayed Jesus, Matthew 26:14-25)

Chat 2: When you feel discouraged, what are some specific things you do to overcome that feeling?

Chat 3: Discover what happened when Paul confronted a sorcerer named Elymas. (The Lord struck Elymas with blindness because he was trying to keep the governor from believing in Jesus, Acts 13:6-12)

Chat 4: Have you heard of Wicca? If so, what is it and what do you think is God's opinion about it?

GRAPPLE TIME: 10-15 MINUTES
Get Ready: Cue the Grapple DVD to the "Plugged In" clip.

Ask kids to get into their Grapple Teams as you pass out paper and pencil. Then lead the entire class in the following:

What is evil? As a team come up with a short definition. Then brainstorm examples of evil that people your age might encounter. See how many you can come up with in just a few minutes.

After three or so minutes, use markers to list kids' ideas on newsprint or butcher paper where everyone can see it.

IN PAIRS
Which of these examples have you encountered, and how did you handle it? Which example would concern you most if you encountered it? Why?

TELL ALL
What do you think are the top three examples of evil most relevant to students your age? How often, on average, do teenagers think about, talk about, or engage in evil? Why does knowing what is and isn't evil matter?

Show the "Plugged In" clip on the Grapple DVD.

I think we can all agree that evil is real, even if we disagree for now on what it is. Some evil looks interesting, even intriguing. Some evil looks downright repulsive and, well, evil. So what does evil have to do with us, with how we live day to day? You and I couldn't do anything truly evil, could we? Today we'll grapple with what the Bible has to say about evil!

GRAPPLE TEAM TIME: 20-25 MINUTES
Break into Grapple Teams. Encourage Grapple Team leaders to check in with kids about their week. Grapple Team leaders will facilitate discussion, using the Grapple Team Guide on pages 114-116. Afterward, students will report what they learned.

GRAPPLE TEAM REPORTS: 10 MINUTES
At the end of Grapple Team Time, match Grapple Teams that chose Option 1 with Grapple Teams that chose Option 2 from page 116. Have teams present their reports. (If you have an uneven number of teams, simply form one group of three teams for the presentations. If you have only two Grapple Teams, simply do the presentations one team at a time.)

GRAPPLE PRAYER AND CHALLENGE: 5 MINUTES
Read the Grapple Prayer options. Have the class choose one prayer option that everyone will do. Allow students time to pray about what they discovered. Then close in prayer.

Get Ready: For Option 1, distribute markers and small pieces of masking tape.

Option 1: Sticky Situations
Write one of your weaknesses on a small piece of masking tape. Put the tape on your arm, leg, or face. Then pray, asking God to be strong in your weakness. Ask God to speak up for you as your enemy tries to hurt you.

Option 2: Power Prayers
Clench your fists tight as you imagine using all your power to maintain control over all the different areas of your life. Talk with God, asking for his powerful perspective, and gradually unclench your fists as you give God control. With your hands open and empty, ask God to fill you with his empowering, life-giving Spirit.

GRAPPLE CHALLENGE

Galatians 1:4-5 says, "Jesus gave his life for our sins, just as God our Father planned, in order to rescue us from this evil world in which we live. All glory to God forever and ever! Amen." Jesus died for us because evil is real and we are surrounded by it in our world. Jesus rescued us so that we can live free from evil. Did you realize that "evil" is "live" spelled backward? That's just it: Doing evil is living backward from what God intends for you.

This week, I challenge you to remember how God calls us to live. Throughout each day, pray that God would fill you with the Holy Spirit and keep you safe from evil.

WEEKLY GRAPPLE CONNECTION
(You can use this as an email template to send to parents)

Grapple Question: Is It Evil?
Kids Learn: The Spiritual World Is Real—So I Will Seek God Only
Dig Into the Bible: Deuteronomy 18:9-22

Witchcraft, psychics, Wicca—there are so many confusing spiritual choices out there. Can you recognize evil around you? Some evil is obvious and looks downright repulsive. But some evil looks interesting—intriguing even. Is it possible for you or your child to recognize if something is truly evil?

Jesus died for us because evil is real and we live in an evil world. Jesus rescued us so that we can live free from evil. "Evil" is "live" spelled backward, and doing evil is living backward from what God intends for us. Ask your child to give you an example of a time he or she was presented with an opportunity to do evil this week (remember, that's anything opposite of God's plan). Maybe a friend suggested that your child tell a "little white lie" or copy a few answers on a homework assignment. Also share an example from your week. Together, pray that God will fill you with the Holy Spirit and keep you safe from evil.

- -

LESSON 11
In your Grapple Team, use this guide to grapple with today's question.

If you've ever seen a psychic/medium depicted on TV or in movies, share what it was like.

IN PAIRS

Do you believe people can communicate with spirits, and if so, where do you think that kind of "power" comes from? How do you feel about psychics telling the future or talking to people's dead friends and relatives?

Read Deuteronomy 4:25; Matthew 15:18-20; and James 1:14-16.

IN PAIRS

What do these verses say about evil—where it comes from and what it does? What examples do these passages give? Given what you read in these verses, do you think the definitions of evil you offered earlier were accurate or inaccurate, and why?

Read Deuteronomy 18:9-14 and Galatians 5:17-21.

On a separate piece of paper, list all the activities these passages describe as evil. Put a dot next to those activities you have been or could potentially be involved in. Does anything on the list surprise you? If so, what, and why? What do these passages say about the influence of someone else on you, and what do you think that means?

Read Luke 4:1-13 and Mark 1:23-28.

What do these passages say about the existence of God's enemy? How did Jesus respond to evil? What can that tell you about how you can respond to the temptation to do evil? What can you learn from these stories about God's power versus the enemy's power?

Before his crucifixion, Jesus prayed for his followers, including you and me.

Read John 17:13-21.

IN PAIRS

Why do you think Jesus prayed this for us? How does it make you feel to know that Jesus prayed for you? What difference could that make in your life this week?

Read Amos 5:14-15 and Ephesians 6:10-18.

Since evil is real, what do these passages say we can do about it? What might that look like on a daily basis?

GRAPPLE TEAM REPORTS

With your team, choose one of the options below to report what you discovered.

Option 1: Text It

Write a 160-word text message that you could send to a friend or family member explaining what you learned today.

Option 2: Relay Report

Discuss some of the big ideas you've learned today. Once you're ready to make your presentation to the other team, line up on one side of the room. Run down to the other end of the room and back. When you return, tell about something you learned today. Then the next person in line runs to the end of the room and back, and reports something else. Continue until everyone has participated.

IS IT EVIL?

1 Peter 3:15
Instead, you must worship Christ as Lord of your life. And if someone asks about your Christian hope, always be ready to explain it.

GRAPPLE CHAT

Chat 1: Find at least one Bible "villain" and what he or she did that was bad.

Chat 2: When you feel discouraged, what are some specific things you do to overcome that feeling?

Chat 3: Discover what happened when Paul confronted a sorcerer named Elymas.

Chat 4: Have you heard of Wicca? If so, what is it and what do you think is God's opinion about it?

GRAPPLE CHALLENGE

This week, remember how God calls us to live. Throughout each day, pray that God would fill you with the Holy Spirit and keep you safe from evil.

NOTES:

_____

_____

_____

_____

_____

_____

_____

_____

_____

CROSSES, CRESCENTS, AND CAPRICORNS

IS IT OK TO ARGUE?

CROSSES, CRESCENTS, AND CAPRICORNS

Is It OK to Argue?
The Point: My Life Will Be a Witness
The Passages: Proverbs 13:10; 18:19; Acts 26:12-29; 2 Corinthians 10:4-5;
Philippians 2:14-15; 2 Timothy 2:23-25; 1 Peter 3:8-17

GET STARTED
Lesson 12. Is It OK to Argue?

GRAPPLE SCHEDULE

5 MINUTES	HANG TIME
10 MINUTES	GRAPPLE CHAT
10-15 MINUTES	GRAPPLE TIME
20-25 MINUTES	TEAM TIME
10 MINUTES	TEAM REPORTS
5 MINUTES	PRAYER & CHALLENGE

SUPPLIES
Bibles, Grapple DVD, DVD player, music CD, CD player, copy of the Grapple
Team Guide for each person, paper, pens or pencils, newsprint or butcher paper,
markers, bull's-eye

BIBLE BASIS FOR TEACHERS
The Passage: 1 Peter 3:8-17
Peter warns Christians about the potential for suffering, and he encourages them
to be prepared for persecution. Peter suggests that to live righteously in the
midst of persecution and opposition from individuals who argue against Christian
philosophy, Christians should remain courageous and continue to acknowledge
Christ as Lord. As we acknowledge Christ, we also express the hope we have in
Jesus and do so with gentleness and respect. Therefore, we ought to respond to
hostility with a gentle and respectful expression of our hope in Jesus Christ. We
have a greater impact when words of gentleness and respect are accompanied
with a lifestyle that matches—actions speak louder than words.

How does this relate to the Grapple Question? This lesson will help students
grapple with the idea of engaging in conversations with atheists, agnostics, and
other people who are hostile toward Jesus and those who follow him. Christians
sometimes perceive atheists and agnostics as having the upper hand when
it comes to apologetics. This lesson will help kids realize that we can engage
atheists and agnostics in intelligent debate. Christians are not living in the
Dark Ages, as some opponents suggest. Most importantly, this lesson will help
students recognize the convincing power of witness. Actions speak louder than
words, so when kids practice what they preach, they'll demonstrate to atheists
and agnostics that they're serious about their beliefs.

How does this connect to Jesus? Jesus promised us the Holy Spirit, and the Holy Spirit gives every Christian the power and authority to explain the hope we have in Christ in a gentle and respectful way (1 Peter 3:15). It isn't enough, however, to just say what we believe. We are instructed to live our life in that truth as well. Peter writes, "Then if people speak against you, they will be ashamed when they see what a good life you live because you belong to Christ" (1 Peter 3:16). Following Jesus requires more than just being able to formulate an argument; it requires dedication to demonstrate our faith in how we live our lives.

GRAPPLE HANG TIME: 5 MINUTES
Play music as kids enjoy snacks and friendship, and then play an opening countdown from the Grapple DVD to wrap up Grapple Hang Time.

GRAPPLE CHAT: 10 MINUTES
Have students form pairs; if you have an uneven number of kids, it's OK to have one trio in the mix. Ask each group to chat about two of the four topics below that relate to today's grapple topic. (Answers in parentheses are samples.)

IN PAIRS
Chat 1: Find one story in the Bible about people fighting over something. (Abram and Lot's herdsmen, Genesis 13)

Chat 2: What was the topic of your last argument? Did that argument have any effect on the relationship between you and the other person?

Chat 3: Discover who met Jesus in a light from heaven and how that meeting changed his life. (Saul, who went from persecuting Christians to being one, Acts 9:1-31)

Chat 4: Do you enjoy watching movies or TV shows that show lawyers and court cases? Why or why not?

GRAPPLE TIME: 10-15 MINUTES
Get Ready: Cue the Grapple DVD to the "Talking the Talk and Walking the Walk" clip.

Lead the entire class in the following:

Think of three topics you feel strongly about—for example, your favorite band, least favorite school subject, and one adventure you'd give anything to try in your lifetime. Pause.

Partner up and choose who will start. Pause. *Starters, choose one of those three topics, and argue with your partner about it. This is an anything-goes conversation.*

In fact, if you hear another argument and want to jump in or bring those people over to your argument, go for it. You'll have one minute to argue before we switch partners and topics. Ready, set, argue!

Repeat as time allows, ensuring that everyone gets to start at least one argument.

IN PAIRS
How often do you think you argue during a typical day? Is that a lot, or is it a reasonable amount? How do you know? Has an argument ever strained a relationship with someone important to you? Explain.

TELL ALL
Did you enjoy this activity, or did it make you uncomfortable? Why? What did you notice about the arguments or about people as they were arguing? Generally, what do your friends argue about? How do you resolve your arguments?

Show the "Talking the Talk and Walking the Walk" clip on the Grapple DVD.

People argue about everything from the seemingly insignificant—their preferred brand of toothpaste or who will take out the trash—to the potentially important—politics, money, religion. Arguments handled well can bring about new perspectives and deeper relationships. Handled poorly, an argument can be destructive. But isn't what you believe worth arguing about? Or are some beliefs so personal that they're off the table? What if someone believes in a totally different religion or no religion at all—can you still be friends? Can you talk about it, even if it leads to an argument? Is it OK to argue? Let's argue, um, rather, discuss that now!

GRAPPLE TEAM TIME: 20-25 MINUTES
Break into Grapple Teams. Encourage Grapple Team leaders to check in with kids about their week. Grapple Team leaders will facilitate discussion, using the Grapple Team Guide on pages 125-126. Afterward, students will report what they learned.

GRAPPLE TEAM REPORTS: 10 MINUTES
At the end of Grapple Team Time, match Grapple Teams that chose Option 1 with Grapple Teams that chose Option 2 from page 126. Have teams present their reports. (If you have an uneven number of teams, simply form one group of three teams for the presentations. If you have only two Grapple Teams, simply do the presentations one team at a time.)

GRAPPLE PRAYER AND CHALLENGE: 5 MINUTES
Read the Grapple Prayer options. Have the class choose one prayer option that everyone will do. Allow students time to pray about what they discovered. Then close in prayer.

Get Ready: For Option 1, affix the bull's-eye to the far wall, and distribute paper to students. For Option 2, distribute paper and make sure students have pens or pencils.

Option 1: Marksman, Markswoman

Make paper airplanes, and take turns throwing the airplanes at the bull's-eye. Walk to wherever your airplane lands and pray to God about one way you miss the mark in your life. Relate what you say to what you learned today.

Option 2: Letter Prayers

Write a letter to Jesus. Tell him what you know is true about him and what you're unsure about; ask for his strength and help in developing a deeper trust in him.

GRAPPLE CHALLENGE

While arguing can harm relationships, knowing what you believe and being willing to share what Christ has done for you might be the tool God uses to bring more people to himself. Just before he ascended into heaven, Jesus said this in Acts 1:8 to his followers: "But you will receive power when the Holy Spirit comes upon you. And you will be my witnesses, telling people about me everywhere."

This week, I challenge you: Each time you leave your house, pray that the Holy Spirit will fill you with power and courage to introduce others to Jesus through your actions and with your words—not in an argumentative way, but with gentleness and respect. And watch what God does!

WEEKLY GRAPPLE CONNECTION
(You can use this as an email template to send to parents)

Grapple Question: Is It OK to Argue?
Kids Learn: My Life Will Be a Witness
Dig Into the Bible: 1 Peter 3:8-17

Do members of your family tend to be the argumentative types—people who defend to the death their choice of toothpaste or which way the toilet paper goes on the holder? People argue about everything and anything, from the seemingly insignificant to the potentially important (politics, money, religion). Arguments handled well can bring about new perspectives and deeper relationships. Handled poorly, an argument can be destructive.

Some things are worth sticking up for, like believing that Christ died for our sins and made a relationship with God possible. But we don't have to argue about that—our actions and the way we live can speak for us. As a family, have each person think of a way they can use their actions to demonstrate their faith to others. While arguing can harm relationships, knowing what you believe and being willing to share what Christ has done for you might be the tool God uses to bring more people to faith.

LESSON 12

In your Grapple Team, use this guide to grapple with today's question.

Draw a large circle on newsprint or butcher paper to represent your team. Choose someone to start, and hand that person a marker. Each person will take a turn writing one thing inside the circle that could be important for you all to agree about and then writing one thing outside the circle that doesn't need agreement. For example, it's important to agree on your team's meeting time, but it wouldn't matter to the others what you have for breakfast.

IN PAIRS

Which was easier to come up with: things you need to agree about or things that you don't care if everyone agrees about? Why? What could that tell you about the things people argue about?

Read Proverbs 13:10 and 18:19.

What do these passages reveal about arguing? If these verses are true, why do people still argue? How have you seen the truth of these verses in your life?

_____

_____

Read 1 Peter 3:8-17.

List Peter's action words in this passage written to Christians. Describe the person pictured here. Would you want that person for a friend? Why or why not? How would this person respond to someone who didn't know about or believe in Jesus? What do you think it means to explain something "in a gentle and respectful way"?

_____

_____

IN PAIRS

Do you know anyone like the person Peter described? If so, what do you enjoy about that person? How are you like or unlike that person? How have you demonstrated your relationship with Jesus to others?

The Apostle Paul, author of the following passages, introduced countless people to Christ.

Read 2 Corinthians 10:4-5; Philippians 2:14-15; and 2 Timothy 2:23-25.

What does Paul say are possible results of arguing? What does he suggest as alternatives to arguing? Summarize Paul's main point in these passages in one or two sentences.

_____

_____

Paul lived what he taught. Take a look at this conversation Paul had with a king.

Read Acts 26:12-29.

What do you notice about Paul's conversation? How did Paul put into practice the ideas he wrote in the passages you read earlier? What can you learn from Paul about talking with people who don't believe in Jesus?

_____

_____

GRAPPLE TEAM REPORTS

With your team, choose one of the options below to report what you discovered.

Option 1: Top 5
Create a Top 5 list of the most important, challenging, or meaningful things you learned today. Be prepared to explain why each item on the list is so important, challenging, or meaningful.

Option 2: Instant Object Lesson
Use whatever you can find around you to create some instant object lessons that explain what you learned today. Get creative!

IS IT OK TO ARGUE?

1 Peter 3:15
Instead, you must worship Christ as Lord of your life. And if someone asks about your Christian hope, always be ready to explain it.

GRAPPLE CHAT
Chat 1: Find one story in the Bible about people fighting over something.

Chat 2: What was the topic of your last argument? Did that argument have any effect on the relationship between you and the other person?

Chat 3: Discover who met Jesus in a light from heaven and how that meeting changed his life.

Chat 4: Do you enjoy watching movies or TV shows that show lawyers and court cases? Why or why not?

GRAPPLE CHALLENGE
This week, pray that the Holy Spirit will fill you with power and courage to introduce others to Jesus through your actions and with your words.

NOTES:

_____

_____

_____

_____

_____

_____

_____

_____

_____